Celebrating Liberation: The Commemoration and Instrumentalisation of the End of the Second World War in Contemporary Czech and Slovak Politics

Vladimír Naxera / Petr Krčál

Celebrating Liberation: The Commemoration and Instrumentalisation of the End of the Second World War in Contemporary Czech and Slovak Politics

Bibliographic Information published by the Deutsche Nationalbibliothek
The Deutsche Nationalbibliothek lists this publication in the Deutsche Nationalbibliografie; detailed bibliographic data is available online at http://dnb.d-nb.de.

Library of Congress Cataloging-in-Publication Data
A CIP catalog record for this book has been applied for at the Library of Congress.

Cover illustration:
© Vladimír Naxera & Petr Krčál

This book was published under the project no. 18-08605S funded by the Czech Science Foundation.

ISBN 978-3-631-84536-3 (Print)
E-ISBN 978-3-631-86280-3 (E-PDF)
E-ISBN 978-3-631-86281-0 (EPUB)
10.3726/b18742

© Peter Lang GmbH
Internationaler Verlag der Wissenschaften
Berlin 2021
All rights reserved.

Peter Lang – Berlin · Bern · Bruxelles · New York · Oxford · Warszawa · Wien

All parts of this publication are protected by copyright. Any utilisation outside the strict limits of the copyright law, without the permission of the publisher, is forbidden and liable to prosecution. This applies in particular to reproductions, translations, microfilming, and storage and processing in electronic retrieval systems.

This publication has been peer reviewed.

www.peterlang.com

Content

Prologue 7

Preface 11

Introduction: The importance of researching public celebrations and commemorations of the past 17

Chapter 1: Politics, history, memory, and commemoration .. 23
History, memory, and national mythology 25
The others and national enemies 32
Political calendars, holidays, commemoration, and *Lieux de Mémoire* 43

Chapter 2: Liberation Festival in the most "American city" in Europe 55
Liberation of Pilsen and Western Bohemia 56
History of (non)celebration and sites of collective memory 58
Festival's organisation and the course of celebrations 64
Narrative structure of the Liberation Festival 69
Liberation 71
Occupation 75

Chapter 3: Slovak National Uprising as a "national treasure" and its annual celebrations in Banská Bystrica 87
Slovak National Uprising 89
History of celebrations and sites of collective memory 92
Organisation and the course of celebrations 98

Narrative structure of the SNU anniversary celebrations 101
Liberation 102
Occupation 105

Conclusion 115

Epilogue 123

List of figures 125

Bibliography 127

Prologue

Pilsen – 1986

We were both born in Pilsen in 1986. In those days, a few years before the fall of Communism, one could not say in public that Pilsen was liberated by American and Belgian troops at the end of the Second World War. The party's official narrative said that Pilsen, just as the rest of Czechoslovakia, was liberated by the Soviets.

Pilsen – early 1990s

Vladimír: Sometime in the early 1990s, I might have been around six years old, I went with my family to an exhibition in the maashaus of the historical building of the Pilsen city hall. Besides other things, there was an illustrated map of the Pilsen centre. The street, which was named Americká třída (American Avenue) after the communist regime fell, had a drawing of a jeep full of American soldiers waving the American flag. I remember asking my parents why there were American soldiers in Pilsen.

Petr: As a little child, I remember going regularly (I guess) to the celebrations commemorating the liberation of Pilsen with my parents. My memories of this event are rather fragmentary: a lot of people and noise, military vehicles, candy floss of a disgusting pink colour. At the same time, I remember the following bit – I remember that during the celebrations, someone said to someone else near me that they were finally enjoying the festivities because nobody believed the talk that the liberators were Soviet soldiers dressed as Americans anyway.

Pilsen – mid-1990s

Vladimír: From the mid-1990s, I already remember the yearly celebrations of the liberation of Pilsen by the American army at the end of the Second World War. One year, in particular, stuck in my mind – our family were spending that weekend at our cottage. Our neighbour was taking his sons on a trip to Pilsen, where a convoy of historical and modern military vehicles would be passing (just like any other year). There were hundreds of military enthusiasts in the city, clad in American but also Czechoslovakian or German historical uniforms. I armed myself with an old Soviet camera for this trip, which used an old film big enough for 36 pictures. I remember the first picture I took being of two men in German uniforms waiting for a tram. With a 36-picture film equipped, I pressed the shutter release perhaps 80 times during that day when we saw, besides the convoy, also a re-enactment of the battle for the church in the central city square. Only back at the cottage did I find out that the film had not been properly placed and that it was empty. Back then, I had no idea that the official name of that event was the Liberation Festival, and I did not realise its historical or ideological proportions. To a 10- or 11-year-old child, it was just a day you could watch tanks.

Pilsen – around 2000

Vladimír: At that time, I played in a youth brass orchestra, which often performed at various festivities. Somewhere around 2000, together with members of Sokol and the Scouts, war veterans, and military enthusiasts, we took part in the parade accompanying the convoy of historical vehicles. The traffic was stopped in the city centre, and the parade passed through the street, crossing the whole centre of Pilsen. We played marching music for the whole two or three kilometres of the parade's route. I remember the weather being extremely hot for early May. I dragged my heavy tuba, and the only part of the celebrations I was aware of was the heat and my wish to be anywhere else.

Banská Bystrica and Komárno – summer 2010

In 2010, Vladimír started his doctoral studies in political science, and Petr entered his last year of master's studies. That summer, our teacher and future colleague Ľubomír Lupták, who influenced our professional interests to a great extent then, took us twice to Slovakia for a field research for his project. It was quite an experience for us as we got to know a "somewhat different political science". At the beginning of the summer holiday, we went to Bratislava, which became our base for shorter trips to Devin and Komárno in particular, where we participated in the unveiling of a statue of the Saints Cyril and Methodius, attended by many political representatives.

Now after some time has passed, we remember mainly the bizarre nature of the situation in Komárno. In the middle of a roundabout surrounded by a grey (post)socialist concrete housing complex, the said statue was unveiled, standing on a massive pedestal, and completely bronze-plated.

We have a different, although similarly curious, experience from Devin where we met a bookseller during the celebrations of the Slovak State, whose stand offered obscure books published by Matica slovenská which presented a "scientific" proof that the Slovaks are an ancient nation because they have had the lactase enzyme allowing them to digest dairy products for over 10,000 years.

At the end of August, we went on the second trip, this time to Banská Bystrica, which we have visited many times since on different occasions. Before the first journey, however, we did not have a completely clear idea of where the city was located and what made it so specific. During our first visit, we observed the celebrations of the Slovak National Uprising anniversary, again with many members of the Slovak political elite present. The research in Komárno and Banská Bystrica resulted in our first paper, among other things, dealing with the political extent of the celebrations.

Pilsen and Banská Bystrica – 2015

For the next few years, we pursued different topics. We kept coming back to Banská Bystrica, which we can say we fell for; not for research, however, but mainly for the conferences held by the local university. At the beginning of 2015, we decided to continue researching the political relevance of public holidays. We managed to get a rather small university project which helped us fund a few days' stay in Banská Bystrica, among other things. Our first trip in 2015 was not a very organised one. We remember that we started wondering if there would be any schedule at all only in the taxi taking us from the Banská Bystrica station to the hotel. In 2015, we also decided to start analyzing the Pilsen Liberation Festival. This did not mean just random observations as in 2010 anymore; in 2015, we started a consistent research of both places, which lasted several years and was completed in 2018–2020 as part of a project provided by the Czech Science Foundation. This book is one of the outcomes of that project.

Pilsen – around 2016

Petr: At that time, me and my girlfriend moved to a flat with a balcony facing the street where the show of military vehicles (from historical to contemporary) passes every year. It was about a week before the event. We invited some of our relatives to the still unfurnished and unrenovated place so that we could watch the convoy from the balcony. My strongest memory from watching the convoy that time is the horrible smell of engines and burnt fuel from the passing vehicles, and me actually looking forward to the show being over and me being able to breathe some fresh air inside the flat.

Pilsen – 2020

Petr: One day between the Christmas Eve and the New Year's Eve, I was coming back home from a late afternoon walk with the pram. It was already dark and snowing lightly. In a park, which serves as one of the places of commemoration and which I pass regularly, I noticed something was different. Candles were burning by the memorial of the Czechoslovakian pilots who fell in the British RAF. That would not be unexpected if the candles were not placed behind the memorial. Out of curiosity, I went to see why the candles were behind the memorial and not in front of it as usual. Right by the backside of the memorial, someone buried their dog shortly after Christmas. A dog that, of course, had nothing to do with the RAF pilots; a dog that probably loved this park and went there regularly for walks with its master.

From my point of view, several functions that this place fulfils due to its location and meaning met at this point: someone (like me) crosses this place every day, sees it as a part of the daily routine, and the memorials placed here are almost invisible. Someone sees the park as the place they go for a smoke from work or the adjacent school. For others, it can be a suitable meeting point. And for some, it is a place of recollection – individual (remembering relatives who died in the Second World War or the dog that died during Christmas) or collective, which then imprints in the national mythology. And all those ways this place is used and the symbolism of it can intersect during the Liberation Festival.

Preface

75 YEARS AGO (on April 25th), a big aerial attack was made on the Škoda Works, the last working arms factory of the Third Reich producing mainly dangerous heavy weaponry and ammunition.[1] The people were warned by a BBC broadcast, but that also gave the German anti-aircraft defence system the chance to prepare. Two bombers were shot down during this mission, and their sad fate is commemorated by memorials in Křimice and Litice. Every year, big and well-attended memorial services are held there, which in fact open the Pilsen Liberation Festival. This year, it couldn't take place,[2] but of course I went to honour the memory of those fallen pilots together with the leaders of the city districts. Because we'll never forget!

—**Martin Baxa** *(mayor of Pilsen, April 25, 2020, published on his official Facebook profile)*

MR STRMEŇ, WE WISH YOU HAPPY BIRTHDAY! Goodness and kindness emanate from Vladko Strmeň[3], an exceptional man from Banská Bystrica who celebrated his 92nd birthday this week. I'm happy he accepted my invitation to the city hall where an exhibition is currently being installed on the occasion of the 76th anniversary of the Slovak National Uprising. Despite his age, Mr Strmeň is always active and passes his knowledge and energy to the young generation. I wished him all the best and good health on behalf of all the inhabitants of Banská Bystrica.

—**Ján Nosko** *(mayor of Banská Bystrica, August 28, 2020, published on his official Facebook profile)*

---

1 We will focus more on the significance of the Škoda Works, its bombing by the American air force, and the consequences and legacy of that bombing later in the section about the Liberation Festival in Pilsen.
2 Most events planned as part of the celebrations were cancelled due to the pandemics.
3 Vladimír Strmeň joined the Slovak National Uprising in 1944 as a 16-year-old combatant. He passed through the whole front during the fighting and eventually joined the 1st Czechoslovak Army Corps, that is, a formation of the Czechoslovak Army in exile, led by the future president Ludvík Svoboda and fighting on the Eastern Front alongside the Red Army.

Pilsen is a relatively big historical and industrial city in the western part of the Czech Republic. Banská Bystrica is located in the middle of a picturesque mountain range in central Slovakia. The two cities are just under 450 kilometres apart by air. If you get on a train in Pilsen at 8 o'clock in the morning and take a lunch break in northern Moravia while changing trains, you reach Banská Bystrica at about half past six in the evening. At first, the two cities do not seem to have anything in common, except for being regional centres in two different Central European countries. However, there is one interesting connection – both cities were the places of events at the final stage of the war which have been publicly celebrated and commemorated till this day and which have gained their place in the political calendars (see Mannová 2019; Hájková et al. 2018) of both countries.

At the end of the war, the area of today's Czech Republic was being liberated from two directions – the Soviet armies advanced from the east and the American armies (with a few Belgian units) from the west. The Soviets and the Americans had agreed on a so-called demarcation line which led north-east of Pilsen (see Lehnerová 2017). Thus, it became the biggest Czech city not liberated by Soviet tanks. However, that fact was ideologically inconvenient between 1948 and 1989, and the liberation of Pilsen has been only celebrated since the fall of Communism.

Banská Bystrica was the centre of the Slovak National Uprising, one of the biggest anti-fascist partisan[4] movements within occupied Europe. Although unsuccessful from the military point of view, the uprising became an important aspect of the Slovak national and political mythology right after the war and has been so (in spite of the ideological changes after the fall of Communism) till today. This event also put Slovakia on the "winning side" after the war because it had distanced itself from the collaborating Slovak State (described in more detail in the chapter on the SNU celebrations).

Many physical places of collective memory (see Nora 1989) can be found in both cities, linked to these events from the final phase of the war. And these places stand at the centre of the annual celebrations commemorating

---

4   "Partisan movement" is a kind of shortcut. First of all, the SNU was the action of one part of the regular Slovak army. After the defeat of SNU, some of them (partisans) continued in a guerilla fight.

both events. The celebrations may be linked to regional or even local history, but from the political (or ideological) point of view, they are relevant to the whole society. That is one of the reasons the celebrations in both cities are attended by important political representatives every year. The SNU is one of the key points of the Slovak historical and constitutional identity; the celebrations of the American involvement in the liberation of a part of the Czech Republic resonate with the Euro-Atlantic orientation of the post-Communist Czech foreign policy. Thus, both of these political celebrations have a significant ideological and identifying aspect, which presents the focus of our research.

We became interested in studying the political aspects of public events towards the end of our master's studies in political science under the influence of Erving Goffman's work, in particular his key piece, *The Presentation of Self in Everyday Life* (Goffman 1956). His approach makes possible an analytic reduction of public events to theatre performances providing a tool for the actors to create and maintain specific situational definitions. As we mentioned earlier, we first encountered the research of public events in 2010; however, we have been researching the celebrations of the Slovak National Uprising anniversary and the Liberation Festival in a more systematic manner since 2015. Our original inspiration by Goffman's work led mainly to our initial interest in the organisational and procedural level of the political aspect of the celebrations, which manifested itself in several texts (e.g. Krčál & Naxera 2011).

From the perspective of dramaturgical politics, the above-mentioned collective ceremonies present a relevant field of research as they provide a platform for the participating politicians who play specific roles in their prepared performances, lean towards certain values and opinions, and use the symbolism of a given event's date, place, and time to support their demands (Alexander 2006, p. 61). Both of the observed political spectacles, which revolve around several physical places of collective memory (see Nora 1989), to a considerable extent linked to a specific form of the politics of dead bodies (see Verdery 1999), that is, the politicisation of human casualties, have a key connection. This post-socialist political necromancy is based on donning a metaphorical cloak of freedom (the Pilsen Liberation Festival carries this value in its name; the tone of the SNU anniversary celebrations, logically, frames them as a celebration of the victory over non-freedom). It is freedom that serves as one of the central collective myths of modern societies (see Barthes 1972; Košťálová 2012), and from this point of view presents a suitable "stage" for the political spectacle to play in the background (see Goffman 1966).

Therefore, as soon as the first year of our systematic research, we also observed the speeches of the attending politicians and other representatives who used the symbolism of the ceremonies to make political requests legitimised by narratives linked to the celebrated historical event. In further research, we gradually shifted the interest in the organisational aspects of an event and its visual analysis to the discourse (re)produced within the delivered speeches, that is, to a content and discourse analysis of textual production. In the assortment of papers, we can link to this stage of our research, the discourse analysis is, however, combined with some dramaturgical aspects of an event (Krčál & Naxera 2015, 2016; Naxera & Krčál 2016a, 2016b, 2016c, 2017a, 2017b, 2019), or performativity elements (Naxera & Krčál 2021). With time, our interest in content and discourse analysis of the textual production by the celebrations' actors prevailed completely and is only marginally complemented by notes on a given event's dramaturgy. This has surfaced in our newer papers (Krčál & Naxera 2019; Naxera & Krčál 2020a, 2020b). The presented book, which results from our six-year-long research, aims at combining those views. Thus, the text is pluralistic from the perspective of theory and methodology (and to a certain extent interdisciplinary, although its core is set in political science).

We would like to express our thanks to several people and institutions here. First of all, to our colleague Ľubomír, whom we already mentioned and who brought us to the research of public events; and to our friends and colleagues with whom we have discussed our research over the years and who gave us valuable feedback – in particular, the historian Miroslav Michela, one of the leading authorities on the SNU and its celebrations; the political scientist Radek Buben; and furthermore, Eliška Poláčková and Alice Koubová, with whom we worked on an interdisciplinary publication on performativity (Koubová & Poláčková 2021) and who helped us improve our grasp of the research from the performative point of view. We also thank Pavla Zákravská for translating our often over-complicated expressions; and, of course, our wives who tolerated our yearly trips to Banská Bystrica. More thanks go to the Czech Science Foundation for providing funds within research project 18-08605S, which made it possible to work on and publish this book but also to finance the last three years of our field research. And last but not least, we thank our alma mater – the Department of Politics and International Relations, University of West Bohemia, which supported our research interests as well.

Introduction: The importance of researching public celebrations and commemorations of the past

Commemorating pivotal historical events is a standard tool for building national mythology and creating collective identity (Hosking & Schöpflin 1997; Hroch 2009; Košťálová 2012; Krasnodebski, Garsztecki & Rüdiger 2012). For that reason, commemoration rituals have a considerable professional attention of various social sciences and humanities; be they nearly mystical narratives relating to a "birth of a nation" or "formation of a state", or modern events, which still represent turning points in the lives of societies, nations or whole continents and their development (see Forchtner 2016; Strukov, Apryshchenko 2018). One such milestone is the Second World War, the most destructive conflict in human history whose legacy has a strong presence in national mythology, collective memory, sacral topography, and political discourse till this day (see Roediger et al. 2019; Biesecker 2002; Pakhomenko & Gridina 2020; Bernstein 2015; Garsztecki 2012; Mironowicz 2012; Grynevych 2012; Sniegon 2017).

Commemorating and remembering the Second World War events plays an important part within European societies in relation to reconciliation[5] and a clear separation from the past. It also serves as a source and manifestation of "learning from the past". One example of that can be how Germany has coped/is still coping with the Second World War history – from numerous sites of memory, trauma sites, and commemoration rituals to the enrichment of the German language with words having a clear meaning and link to the event (Gilbert 2020, p. 17; cf. Kulawik & McLoughlin 2020). Considering the meaning of the Second World War to Europe (and the whole world), the celebrations of this conflict's end have a strong tradition in Europe – and that does not mean just the probably best-known military parade taking place in Moscow. The end of the war is commemorated in different ways in different

---

5 In the sense of "overcoming" past wrongs, accepting the roles of "victims" and "aggressors", and commencing a new stage of relations between the involved parties (Gilbert, McLoughlin & Munro 2020; D'Orsi 2015).

European countries, taking into consideration regional or local specifics, culture, and history.[6] Naturally, this fact is reflected in specialised literature, and the general meaning, as well as specific examples of commemoration, reconciliation, and rejuvenation rituals and their location by trauma sites and sites of memory, are a popular subject of research[7] (see e.g. Cingerová & Dulebová 2020; Gilbert, McLoughlin & Munro 2020; Violi 2012; Sendyka 2016; Wingfield 2000; Wittenberg 2015; Zombory 2017; Krasnodebski, Garsztecki & Rüdiger 2012; Szaló 2017).

With this book, we aspire to join this extensive tradition within social sciences and humanities and contribute with an analysis of two specific examples of public festivities (see Šima 2017; Musilová 2014) relating to the events and legacy of the final stage of the Second World War. The first of these commemoration events is the Liberation Festival in Pilsen (Czech Republic), a public event lasting several days celebrating the liberation of Pilsen in 1945 by the American army and contributing Belgian units. The second observed event is the celebration of the Slovak National Uprising anniversary, also held annually in Banská Bystrica (Slovakia). In 1944, it was Banská Bystrica that became the centre and headquarters of the uprising, which spread over a considerable portion of the Slovak State. Despite its lack of military success, it became a fixed part of the Slovak national mythology, and its commemoration became one of the most important holidays in the Slovak political calendar (e.g. Michela 2020a; Mannová 2008; Miháliková 2005; Lipták 1995).

We can find many substantial differences between the two celebrations[8] – both on the level of the celebrated event's symbolism and in the form of the

---

6   And reflecting the events immediately following the war in particular. In countries with the post-communist experience, the celebrations of the end of the Second World War are specific because, at the same time, they are connected to a symbolic distancing from the communist regime and a reframing/restructuring of the narrative carried by commemoration rituals, which is evident in the example of the events we follow as well (see Švecová 2020, on a general level Tomczuk 2016).

7   Which, of course, is not limited to the Second World War conflict but generally covers crucial and/or traumatic events and their incorporation within the collective memory/collective forgetting of a given society.

8   We can find more differences in the extent to which these topics are covered by academic literature. While the Slovak National Uprising and the celebrations thereof are topics frequently occurring in the Slovak historiography, the

festivities. We can illustrate that here at the beginning on two examples. As already mentioned, both celebrations revolve around the central idea of freedom which is greatly mythologised, reified, and commodified. However, the sources of that freedom are different. While the Pilsen Liberation Festival presents a ritualised celebration of freedom given externally, the festivities in Banská Bystrica celebrating the Slovak National Uprising are about freedom (or an attempt at freedom) gained internally, that is, from within the society that rose against an occupying and collaborating regime. Thus, we discover different directions from which "freedom came" (from the outside "on the tracks of American tanks" or from the inside "on the barrels of partisan machine guns"). While those remembered during the celebrations of the SNU are the Slovak partisans above all, it is the American army in the Pilsen festival.

As far as the organisation is concerned, we can observe differences in the dramaturgy and location of the SNU and LF festivities as such. The SNU celebrations are concentrated around a single site of memory – the Monument of the SNU and the museum inside. The festivities thus take place around a monument built as a reminder of the event whose location and architecture (the building has two sections separated by free space to portray a divide, a tragic story of war seen from two sides; we will get to the monument again later) make it an artificial site of memory (in a significantly nationalised manner, see Szaló 2017, pp. 150–152) the Slovak National Uprising. The symbolism of this place, a specific time, and a specific event (see Alexander 2006) is also considerably instrumentalised during the SNU festivities by the political participants who use the SNU mythology, genius loci, and political necromancy[9] towards a ritualised legitimisation of their political visions, towards the creation of binary categories of good versus evil, friend versus enemy, and so forth. And as is the case of the Pilsen Liberation Festival, during the SNU festivities, too, these can be visions and demands completely unrelated to the

---

liberation of Pilsen and its commemoration appear only in a handful of existing texts.

9 Using the term "political necromancy", we loosely develop the concept of the "political life of dead bodies" arising from the work of Katherine Verdery (1999). We will revisit it again later.

celebrated event (e.g. using the SNU's legacy to distinctly refuse to assist refugees during the so-called migrant crisis). However, the celebrations in Pilsen are different in their structure – there is no single focal point, the festivities take place for several days in different places in the city and its surroundings. The individual venues where tributes are paid and the various parts of the festival happen are usually some of Pilsen's many memorials and monuments. We consider the shared characteristics of the two events as well as their differences to be a suitable foundation for a deeper comparison of these commemoration acts.

Our primary goal and ambition is to contribute to the debate about political instrumentalisation of the past and political formation of history by means of two case studies resulting from our six-year-long systematic field research. We focus on the manner in which public commemorations of historical events are (mis)used and instrumentalised by today's political elite. The six-year-long research mentioned above was done systematically during 2015–2020 as semi-participant observations of the individual events during both celebrations. However, 2020 was specific – due to the worldwide COVID-19 pandemic, the actual May festivities in Pilsen were cancelled and replaced by a programme containing a whole range of on-line events.[10] The celebrations in Banská Bystrica took place, but in view of the travelling restrictions during the pandemics, we could not attend in person. However, we worked with a TV recording of the main part of the ceremony.

The research of public events and holiday celebrations will necessarily have an interdisciplinary scope – although our own research is based on political science, politics meets history, sociology, theatre studies, anthropology, and memory studies. It is pluralistic in the subject as well as methodology and theory. Thus, the whole research and the subsequent presented publication are not bound by a single strictly followed and fetishised method

---

10 That in itself demonstrates the importance of the festival – not even during the culminating spring wave between April and May was it cancelled completely. Although moved to the on-line sphere, the event was preserved at least partially. Events to pay tribute (at least in a restricted form without speeches and audience) took place as well (see the quotation of mayor Baxa at the beginning of the Preface).

and theory. The pluralistic approach is evident in the various means of data extraction (e.g. observation, medial coverage, interviews) and the numerous ways of analyzing and interpreting said data (dramaturgic analysis, content analysis, discourse analysis, etc.). If necessary, the individual steps of the research will be elaborated in the following chapters. Our book aspires to be a standard academic text in all its aspects but also a readable material accessible to a wider range of readers. Unless necessary, we do not wish to encumber the text with methodological notes and specialised jargon.

The book is comprised of three main parts, which gradually take the reader through our research. The first part introduces general themes and theoretical concepts that we use. The chapter thus connects several perspectives which helped us grasp the research – from highlighting the political aspect of history interpretation and the clash between history and memory through forming *the others*, the relevance of public events and political calendars to individual concepts like the "political life of dead bodies" (Verdery 1999) or "sites of collective memory" (Nora 1989). We aim to be as brief and clear as possible when introducing these concepts; the purpose is to frame our research.

The two central chapters are then devoted to the individual celebrations. Although both chapters have parallel structures (we focus on an introduction of the celebrated events, the history of remembering them, the dramaturgical aspect of the festivities, the participating actors, the analysis of public speeches, on connecting the celebrations to a wider political and ideological frame around them, and the associated facts and factors), the specifics of the individual cases need to be stressed as well. In the conclusion, we summarise the main contributing points of our research and suggest further potential directions to explore.

Chapter 1 Politics, history, memory, and commemoration

Interpreting and staging the past is an integral part of politics in its different forms (e.g. Assmann 1999, 2006, 2007; Assman 2001; Krasnodebski, Garsztecki & Ritter 2012; Mayer & Vašíček 2008; Olick, Vinitzky-Seroussi & Levy 2011). Selected historical events that are given greater importance have often been a subject of political conflict. They often enter the process of formation of political identities, creation of ideological frameworks, as well as the discourse of political parties and other actors, or "the political" as such. At the same time, it is a sphere that has long been addressed by public and state institutions affected by these political conflicts and whose control is sought by political entities operating with a certain conception of the past in their ideological and programmatic framework (e.g. Hájková et al. 2018). Political and social order is thus closely connected with the desired shape of history, which is often reified in the form of physical places serving as its symbols (Verdery 1999, p. 6).

We intend to analyse these processes in more detail in this chapter, which presents the frameworks and concepts we use in individual case studies. Our goal is to define the concepts we work with and place our research in a broader academic discussion. Although we draw on literature and approaches of many fields, history in particular, the text is written from political scientists' perspective and mainly for a political science readership. The price for this practice is a certain compaction and abbreviation of some arguments. However, it should be noted that this section primarily provides a basis for subsequent studies. The whole chapter is written largely on a general and theoretical level and also interspersed with several examples, mainly from the Czech and Slovak setting. These examples have an illustrative purpose and help build the context necessary for understanding the case studies, especially by readers who are not familiar with Czech and Slovak political developments and realities. For this reason, some of the given examples, which we consider highly relevant, are presented in more detail (for instance, the perception of Germans and Germany in the Czech-Slovak environment). Even so, they are (due to the actual objective of the text) conceived rather compactly, and the often complicated discussions are intentionally outlined schematically.

In this section, we want to emphasise, among other things, certain differences between the Czech and Slovak examples. Although for most of the 20th century, the Czechs and Slovaks shared the same state, this state's existence was interrupted by the events of the Second World War. In the autumn of 1938, Slovakia gained autonomy, and the state was renamed from Czechoslovakia to Czecho-Slovakia. In the spring of 1939, just before the occupation of the Czech lands by the German army and the declaration of the Protectorate of Bohemia and Moravia, Slovakia declared independence and the Slovak state was proclaimed.

The coexistence in the joint state had also been disrupted even before these events by many factors – somewhat colonial attitudes of the Czechs towards the Slovaks and Slovakia, manifested in evident Czech dominance, present since the establishment of Czechoslovakia,[11] or, for example, different process of forming the modern nations and of the national revival in the 19 century (cf. Lipták 2007). The Czech and Slovak nations, in the modern sense, were formed under different conditions of two different parts of the Habsburg monarchy and in confrontation with different dominant nations[12] (cf. Hroch 1999; Křen 2005). Even these differences, which we will encounter on the following pages, affected the current politics.

Therefore, this chapter will introduce several topics, one by one. We will first focus on the relationship between two important concepts – history and memory. They allow us to follow up with national mythology as we introduce various forms of national myths. The shaping of national history often occurs by defining oneself against groups that are commonly perceived

---

11 This colonial approach penetrated the national mythology of both Czechs and Slovaks in the form of a civilisation mission proclaiming the paternalism of the developed Czech nation towards weaker and backward Slovaks (Mannová, 2019, p. 60). This myth then shaped some lines in the relationship between the Czechs and Slovaks, and escalated with the disintegration of the joint state.
12 However, due to social and political demand, the past was interpreted in a way that gave the sense of continuity and unity of the Czechs and Slovaks based on the search for shared roots in Great Moravia, Hussites, mutual suffering and oppression by historical enemies, and later in a shared sentiments of the Munich betrayal (Mannová 2019, p. 65).

as *the others* – the next section will pay particular attention to such groups. Finally, we will focus on the importance of historical turning points for shaping national and political calendars, on festivities and celebrations of these historical events, on the so-called *Lieux de Mémoire* (Nora 1989), around which these celebrations often revolve. Regarding the concept of the sites of memory mentioned above, similarly important for our point of view is the concept of the politics of dead bodies (Verdery 1999). These individual parts will be then connected within a consistent framework which we refer to as the post-socialist political necromancy, a perspective through which we grasp our several years of research.

History, memory, and national mythology

The political significance of history is indisputable[13] (cf. Anušauskas 2012). A belief about a shared past serves as one of the key points for creating a collective identity (cf. Anderson 2016). Among other things, this is often based on a convenient interpretation of national history in the form of a *usable past*, which enters the textbooks as the "ultimate truth" (cf. Hroch 2009). History shaped in such a manner reflects several factors – from the dominant ideology through a temporary need for "creating history" and (re)interpreting it to the worldview of a specific author (cf. Abăseacă 2018; Benazzo 2017; Lentin 2009; Wittenberg 2015). At one point, there may be several different interpretations standing against each other – these ideas of the past are thus competitive with each other (cf. Michela 2008).

Apart from the competing interpretations of the past, we can also point out that the state apparatus and its ideological components (cf. Althusser 2014) primarily frame history as political[14] (Lipták 2007, p. 6), as a series of interrelated political events. From this perception of the past, national myths derive depicting national heroes, martyrs, allies and, of course, enemies (cf. Lipták 2007; Rak 2018; Chlup 2020). How history is instrumentalised

---

13 And how it passes through the political filter of what is worth remembering and what is forgotten. History is always formed politically, in the sense that only certain narratives, certain stories, are enforced, and thanks to this filtering of the past, only some histories are "significant".
14 For this reason, it is possible to perceive history and political science as two closely intertwined and complementary disciplines (cf. McLean 2010).

and interpreted, and what narrative it represents, thus serves as one of the tools for the formation of national (collective) as well as individual identity (Mannová 2019, p. 11). After all, the examples of changes in the interpretation of the liberation of Pilsen and the Slovak National Uprising, on which we will focus in individual chapters, are a good demonstration of such instrumentalisation of history.

The process of (re)shaping history is visible especially in the case of a qualitative change of the political regime (cf. Machcewicz 2012; Verdery 1999, p. 6) and its ideological framework (cf. Etkind 2013). In the Czech and Slovak context, the 20th century brought several waves of reinterpretation of the official reading of history. Major turning points were reached, among others, with the foundation of Czechoslovakia, the Second World War and the establishment of the Slovak State, the liberation, the formation and collapse of the communist regime, the processes of the Prague Spring, or the dissolution of Czechoslovakia and formation of national states of the Czechs and Slovaks (see Lehnerová 2017; Lipták 2007; Mannová 2008; Tomczuk 2016; Wingfield 2020).[15]

However, even without a transformation of the political regime's formal framework, significant changes in the interpretation of history can occur, bringing new forms of identity conflicts. That can be illustrated with the transformation of discussions in the Czech Republic throughout the whole post-Communist period. The allegedly exemplary transition (e.g. Musil 1992; Dvořáková & Kunc 1994) made it seem that the Czech conflicts over the past would be concerned mainly with the question of the previous regime (Mayer 2009) and not older matters, not to mention other aspects of identity (Holy 1996). The issues of the state border, foreign policy orientation, or attitude towards ethnic, national and religious minorities did not really seem to matter in the homogeneous Czech Republic, a country based on inter-elite pro-Western consensus. However, the rise of identity politics and Fukuyama's "demands for dignity" and "politics of resentment"

---

15 Such a reinterpretation can be seen in the case of dealing with the post-war past, the expulsion of Germans from border areas and the ideologically controlled oblivion to the German ethnic group, which, in some regions, made up the majority of the population before the displacement (cf. Wyss 2020). We will get to the question of the Germans below.

(Fukuyama 2018) emerged in the Czech Republic at the end of the first decade of our century. Apart from the traditional political disputes over the past associated with the "former regime", debates over other historical periods appeared, among other things, on account of the so-called "eight anniversaries" (e.g. Randák 2008; Michela 2008; Sniegon 2017; Bureš 2019). The prevailing illusory consensus had been broken, and conflicts over the past had been linked in various ways to existing political cleavages, in some cases completely transforming them, in other cases having an effect outside this framework. Simultaneously, for the first time in the Czech Republic, the cultural left spoke up more strongly, presenting their understanding of history which replaced, or in other cases reformulated, some of the postulates of the illusory consensus whose supporters agreed with the reformulation or turned away from the existing narrative and adopted the traditionalist version of identity politics (e.g. Slačálek 2010; Kopeček 2011). In addition to the clash between the left and the right, cultural and identity conflicts within the right and within the left have intensified in recent years, whereas the dispute over the interpretation of history within different ideologies plays a significant role within these conflicts.

In these processes, historians play a significant political role (cf. Michela 2014, 2017). Apart from historians, the notion of society's collective history is passed on by institutions and actors that can be seen as the so-called ideological state apparatuses (see Althusser 2014), that is, the mass media, the school system, various cultural and political elites, and last but not least, the family. The *usable past* (re)produced by these actors can be seen in this process in various cases – for instance, in selecting historical events that would be presented as pivotal. As has been mentioned, history is presented primarily as political. The Slovak historian Ľubomír Lipták elaborated this with a metaphor comparing history to a self-service from which everyone takes what they "crave" and what is convenient (Mannová 2019, p. 9; cf. Lipták 2008). This metaphor was then updated by Elena Mannová, who points out that thanks to the development of the Internet and the arrival of social networks, history has transformed from an outdated self-service to a supermarket. Supermarket, in which the past becomes a commodity that everyone can find, modify, decontextualise, and then instrumentalise to fulfil their own goals, however defined (Mannová 2019, p. 9).

Therefore, the past is being used as a political instrument that helps to support future demands with suitable arguments. Historical memory is always constituted and legitimised with respect to the present (and the future) (Hroch 2003). In this regard, it is appropriate to set two different concepts side by side – history and memory (which can be individual or collective; cf. Halbwachs 1994, 1997).

They are two sides of the same coin – the effort of grasping the past. They complement each other, benefit from each other, yet they stand on different foundations. Memory[16] can be defined as the "infinite present", a process of remembering and forgetting, evoking the timeliness of one's stories over and over again through repeated rituals. History and memory are associated with various physical places that allow the collectivity to be defined and anchored in time and space – a process which we will address in one of the following subchapters. These places serve as strongholds for history, although the various commemoration events and other rituals held at these places with the participation of the whole collective point mostly to memory. In any case, there is an apparent connection between the past, the present, and the future (cf. Gurrey & Munro 2020; Košťálová 2012; Moshenska 2020; Violi 2012; Zombory 2017).[17]

---

16 Memory can be well illustrated with the examples of our childhood memories presented in the Prologue. They adequately demonstrate the distance between memory and history.

17 We can illustrate the difference between history and memory with discussions on the nature of the former communist regime (cf. Mayer 2009). After the fall of Communism, the framing of the communist regime as "bad" and even "criminal" (based on the adopted law) prevailed in the Czech setting. Sometimes, there is a search for positive features of the former regime, but these tendencies are often referred to as "relativisation of the crimes of communism", mainly by the so-called winners of privatisation. It is this process that fully exposes the conflict between history and memory, between the role of historians and old-timer witnesses (cf. iROZHLAS 2020). In 2020, there was a debate within Czech academic, political and media circles over the conflict of opinion between the historian Michal Pullmann, one of the leading experts on the social history of the communist regime (e.g. Pullmann 2008, 2011), and the journalist Michal Klíma. The conflict concerned Pullmann's research and claims about the partial democratic features of the communist regime and that a large part of society actively or passively supported the regime for reasons other than fear (for instance, objective improvements in living standards as compared to the pre-Communist

Among other things, rituals associated with these places help to reproduce various myths. This brings us to the role of myth and mythology in shaping collective identity. A myth can be a narrative or a story that relates to a shared destiny, thus uniting the community members. This unifying function of the myth is provided mainly because (national) myths are a set of simplified and stereotyped narratives (Rak 2018, p. 2). While (national) history is a synthesizing narrative, individual national myths are episodes within the historical synthesis (Hroch 2009, p. 190). From this perspective, myths are a tool for creating images of the past through collective memory. However, mythological concepts are unstable – they can (as well as memory) alternate, form, and disappear, which is a result of their historical nature (Barthes 1972).

Individual myths are often associated with war operations (whether lost or won), significant historical turning points (such as occupation, liberation, formation of a state, etc.), or outstanding historical figures ("national heroes" as well as "national villains"; Randák & Koura 2008; Rak 2018). Apart from a number of these minor sacralisation myths (Hroch 2009, pp. 195–198) highlighting partial events/personalities, which we will address later in this chapter since they form a basis for political and national calendars (Hájková et al. 2018), there are plenty of more complex myths used in the study of national histories. These relate, in addition to partial

---

period). Klíma, whose family was persecuted by the communist regime, defined himself against these conclusions of historical research in an exemplary manner from the position of a witness who has a certain memory of the regime and did not accept the results of scientific research incompatible with his own memory. Around this discussion grew a broader academic-socio-political debate in which Pullmann was described as a "revisionist" and a "neo-Marxist" (this strange concept has recently become a common label for ideologically uncomfortable opponents; cf. Busbridge, Moffitt & Thorburn 2020; Slačálek 2018). When the students of the Faculty of Arts of the Charles University, where Pullmann is the Dean, sided with him, Klíma sent them an open letter (see Klíma 2020) in which he de facto continued with the conflict between memory and history – according to Klíma, students should not be getting the picture of the communist regime based on reading history papers of American or French authors, they should draw their own conclusions from archival sources or interviews with the regime witnesses.

events, to the overall narrative anchoring and confirming the collective identity (cf. Košťálová 2012). The myth of beginning is one of them.

The modern national myth was often built on older, medieval and early modern myths, sometimes even returning to the already forgotten pre-modern myths – it did not take them over completely but modified them. This is especially true of the myth of beginning, which played a key role mainly during modern nations' formation. The ancientness of the "nation" was a popular argument in pre-modern times (and remains so to this day – see the mention of Devin in the Prologue, or a quote from former Slovak President Gašparovič later in this chapter). A good example is the Czech medieval myth of the origin of peaceful agricultural immigrants, which was gradually cultivated into the myth of the Slavic democratic easy-going character, the exact opposite of authoritarian and violent Germans or Hungarians (Hroch 2009, p. 192; Lipták 2007, p. 7). In Slovakia, this myth has long been associated with references to the thousand-year oppression (cf. Lupták 2008) and the loss of statehood (see below). Thus, it can be stated that the formation of national mythology and the (often artificially) derived traditional stereotypes and patterns of behaviour (easygoing character, aggressive German, Czech craftsmanship, ancient Slovak nation) are necessary to anchor the "nation" and "state" in the time continuum in order to evoke the feeling that these are essential and timeless structures (cf. Hobsbawm & Ranger 2012; Strážay 2005).[18]

From the perspective of this text, some other complex myths need to be mentioned: mainly, the myth of the Golden Age dealing with the most prosperous periods in the nation's existence, and the myth of national catastrophe or national trauma that can end the Golden Age. After the catastrophe, there comes the Dark Age (the so-called myth of the Dark Age),

---

[18] This method of (re)inventing history can be illustrated on one of the fundamental pillars of the Czech historical tradition – the mythological story of Jan Hus at the Council of Constance and his death for the truth. This narrative has changed historically; initially, it celebrated German Protestants. In the 19th century, under the influence of national revivalist tendencies, the theological truth became part of the national narrative, and later the social and political narrative. In the form of "Havel's" and "Masaryk's" motto "Truth prevails", it has been influencing the perception of the Czech people to this day (Mannová 2019, p. 36).

the opposite of the Golden Age. The Dark Age as an unfavourable period of the nation's evolution can be ended by the national revival, which is associated with the myth of regeneration of the nation (cf. Smith 1997; Košťálová 2012, pp. 120–130).

As we have already mentioned, one of the central myths is the myth of freedom, reified by both commemoration events (cf. Krčál & Naxera 2019). Freedom is a concept that has its place in various political (or more generally, ideological) systems and is often adopted as a value across the political spectrum, although its interpretations can differ (cf. Berlin 1969; Cohen 1989, p. 226; Rawls 2006; Schwarzmantel 2008, p. 54).

Nevertheless, the myth of freedom fits into the above-suggested structure of the "Golden Age – catastrophe – Dark Age – national revival – Golden Age" myths. Freedom is one of the attributes of the Golden Age. At the same time, it can be ended by occupation, which is linked with the myth of catastrophe or trauma. The following liberation, which is the source of a new phase of the Golden Age, is then associated with the myth of revival. Occupation and liberation (and their carriers, i.e., the metaphorical characters of the "occupier" and "liberator") can thus be understood as partial myths associated with the central myth of freedom, and they will play an essential role in our subsequent analysis.

Different perceptions of these myths and roles are also noteworthy – what is a Golden Age for one, may be a Dark Age for another (for instance, the period of Communism in the Czech and Slovak case). This is, after all, a topic that we discussed in one of our previous studies in relation to the annual SNU celebrations (see Naxera & Krčál 2016c). The perception of myths and their specific narratives also change over time, for example, based on the ideological framework's transformations. Similarly, a hero or a liberator for one may be a traitor and occupier for another (Hroch 2009; Krčál & Naxera 2019). With regard to public celebrations of historical events, we can say that the symbolism of the event, time, and place (Alexander 2006, p. 61) can be used for producing these binary labels ("this is the occupier" and "this is the liberator") by an actor participating in the ritual that reifies the given myths. Formation and reification of these opposite meanings are an inherent part of politics (cf. Schmitt 1932). The analysis of these processes is an essential component of the two included case studies. In them, we will observe who and in what way is constructed as a (national) friend or enemy. This construct is inseparably linked to the concept of *the others*.

The others and national enemies

We have already come across the fact that a nation (and its history) is often constructed against *the others*. Collective identity is usually formed within relation to someone who is "different" and not part of our collectivity (cf. Eriksen 2010).[19] Therefore, the relationship towards others is necessary for the construction of our own self – construction of us (cf. Hroch 2009). Although there are many concepts of *the others* (e.g. a guest, a stranger, a neighbour), the most common idea is *the other* as *enemy*.[20] In this case, the relationship towards *the other* is realised through positive autostereotypes and primarily negative heterostereotypes, which constitute a basis for the ethnic vision of the world. In this way, we consolidate the Us identity because we attribute negative qualities to *the other*, making our group's positive qualities stand out in comparison. From a historical perspective, heterophobia/xenophobia undoubtedly prevails over philoxenia. Homogenisation, that is, seeing *the others* exclusively in the plural and as homogeneous groups, not as independent individuals, automatically leads to depersonalisation (*others* do not have names; *others* are all the same), and may ultimately lead to dehumanisation (*others* are not even humans). The disturbing anonymity of *the others* evokes a sense of danger within our own group, leading to a conclusive codification of *the others* as the *enemy*.

Defining *the others*, who are not just a group beyond our collectivity, but are seen as an enemy, has far-reaching political implications. The image of national enemies tends to be related to events and phenomena that are often understood as a national trauma or a Dark Age – possibly a genocide, military defeat, occupation (e.g. Smith 1997). All sorts of feelings of historical injustice can be blended with current politics. A hundred-year-old

---

19 Regarding the formation of collective identity in relation to *the others*, Eriksen (2006) uses the apt metaphor of the nation as an "inverted refrigerator". Similarly, to the negative stereotypisation of *the others*, nations (or any other object of collective identity) create heat and a warm atmosphere inside and produce coldness towards the outside.
20 For the concept of *enemy*, see, for example, Nečasová (2020).

event can thus become the basis for current hatred, which can be a good commodity from a political perspective.

For this reason, reconciliation rituals are crucial for overcoming historical injustices and for a symbolic closure. In these rituals, it is essential to explicitly identify the actors responsible for the wrongdoings as well as the victims of these events. The perpetrators admit their guilt (possibly followed by the process of exculpation), and in case of a reconciliation ritual, the victims forgive them (or accept their guilt without the process forgiveness that is replaced with the act of punishment) (cf. Auerbach 2004; Esterling, John-Hopkins & Harding 2020). These rituals can take various forms – from a one-time political act through annual public events held at a symbolic place to embedding reconciliation into the sacralised topography of a city/landscape by building a site of memory associated with the event. If these processes do not occur and the "old grievances" are not symbolically closed, they may be repeatedly instrumentalised by political actors who use them whenever they need to "play the national enemy card".

How these groups, historically framed as enemies, feature in today's politics can be illustrated with a couple of examples of contemporary Czech political situation. After all, all these mentioned groups play a significant role in the narratives created around the festivities we study.

The category of national enemies is, of course, an escalated version of *the others*. *The others* are used as a point of reference more frequently, as illustrated by the example of the Czech nation. Given how the Czech nation constituted itself during the 19th century, the Germans are naturally the most important *others*. From the beginning of the 16th century, the Czech lands were part of the Habsburg Monarchy, and the modern process of national revival was led mostly against German cultural, political and economic supremacy (cf. Müller 2002; Křen 2005). The perception of a German as an enemy remained to some extent not only after the establishment of Czechoslovakia in 1918 but also long after the collapse of the communist regime in 1989. It was fuelled by events such as the Munich Agreement and the loss of the so-called Sudetenland in 1938, or the occupation and the period of the Protectorate of Bohemia and Moravia in 1939–1945. As Ladislav Holy (1996, passim) points out, for a large part of the Czech society, a German does not relate to the image of a scientist or a philosopher, but rather to the image of an aggressor, oppressor and warlord.[21] For that reason, with the changes in the foreign policy and economic directions of the Czech Republic in the 1990s and with the German capital entering the Czech milieu, many people started to assume that when Germany did not succeed at conquering the Czechs militarily, they will do so economically. Similar negative references to the influence Germany has on the Czech Republic have lasted until today. They can be illustrated, for instance, with a Facebook status of Lubomír Volný, one of the former Deputies of the extreme-right and populist party Freedom and Direct Democracy, who, at the beginning of 2019, wrote the following: *"By accepting Euro, the Czech Republic would confirm the German victory in the Second World War"*. At the same time, there are voices coming from the nationalist scene speaking against Germany not only regarding the economic supremacy but also against the notion of Germany dominating the European Union, supporting the immigration into Europe. In particular, Chancellor Angela Merkel is presented in certain Czech political circles as the evil bringing ruin to the European civilisation.

Germany and the Germans are often a reference point of an own nationalist perception of the Czech state and nation as an active historical entity whose natural development was interrupted by several discontinuities that, nevertheless, can be undone (see Holy 1996, passim). These discontinuities are usually associated with the German influence. First of such disruptions is the Battle of White Mountain (1620)[22] that, according to the prevailing

---

21 This is also reflected in popular culture. We can mention, for example, *Krakonošské pohádky* (Krakonoš fairy tales) – TV series designed as children's bedtime stories. Krakonoš is a mythical protector of the Czech Krkonoše Mountains (or the Giant Mountains), which were historically inhabited by a large German population. The central motif of the series from the mid-1970s, still popular today, is the conflict between Trautenberg, a villainous German landowner, and his Czech groomsmen and servants, whom Krakonoš helps. The opposition is portrayed not only as a class conflict (based on the ideological demand of the time), but also a conflict of nationalities – the name Trautenberg only emphasises the landowner's German origin.

22 Including the battle in national mythology also resulted from the process of creating a desirable interpretation of the past. From the historians' perspective, the battle was rather an insignificant skirmish, which was not decided by a crushing defeat on the battlefield, but by the fact that part of the army did not

socio-cultural narrative, ended the hopes of the anti-Habsburg Bohemian Revolt with their defeat. In the next period, another discontinuity came, this time in the form of Recatholisation and Germanisation of Czech regions (viz Koldinská 2001). This was eventually undone by the establishment of the Czechoslovak state in 1918 and the enactment of wide anti-German legislation (for instance, the revocation of nobility and land reform that led to land expropriation of noble families – the reform was indeed outlined as an atonement for the White Mountain), by not allowing the Czechoslovak Germans to contribute to the constitution of a new state, or by marginalizing them in the political scene of interwar Czechoslovakia. On the other hand, it must be said that a number of German political currents supported the existence of the Czechoslovak state in which they actively participated. One example is the German Social Democratic Party, which was a member of several Czechoslovak governments. At the same time, we should mention the openly anti-systemic and pro-Nazi Sudeten German Party that won the most votes in the 1935 elections among all parties in the country. Another discontinuity was marked by the Munich Agreement in 1938 and a decision made by the European powers that resulted in the loss of the Sudetenland to Germany – historical borderlands settled by German colonists for a thousand years. The Sudetenland was annexed to Germany, and the Czech residents were expelled. In the spring of 1939, the rest of the Czech territory was seized, and the Protectorate of Bohemia and Moravia was established, starting the period of the German occupation. After the liberation in 1945, there comes another atonement for the injustices made by Germany in the form of the ratification of the Beneš decrees applying the principle of collective guilt, after which the German population (not only in Sudetenland, but anywhere in Czechoslovakia) was deprived of their property and citizenship, and consequently expelled[23]

---

receive their pay and left before the battle (Mannová 2019, p. 37). However, this interpretation does not contain the elements of the myth of sacrifice or the myth of defeat and being conquered by *the other*. Therefore, it was modified for the needs of national mythology.

23 In the Czech public discourse, there has long been a major controversy over whether this act should be framed as "expulsion" or a "forced removal".

to Germany, often very brutally (Portmann 2018; Tampke 2003, pp. 73–93).[24]

Discussion on this topic was initiated again after the collapse of the communist regime (see Houžvička 2005), contemplating the Sudetenland history and the legitimacy of the Beneš decrees. At the level of politics, the issue was resolved by means of bilateral agreements in the 1990s (Tampke 2003, pp. 149–150)[25]. However, despite generally good German-Czech relations, it reappeared in the highest level of politics several times. For example, in October 2009, then-President Václav Klaus enforced an exception from the Charter of Fundamental Rights of the EU for the Czech Republic to prevent – according to his words – the annulment of the Beneš decrees by the European Courts. Regardless of this case, it was usually the extreme-right or extreme-left actors[26] who attacked Germany in relation to the Sudetenland and the Beneš decrees and who also often criticised the activities of the Sudetendeutsche Landsmannschaft (Sudeten German Homeland Association) led by Bernd Posselt. The question of the Munich Agreement, the Sudetenland and the Beneš decrees has become an integral part of public discussion. According to investigations by the Public Opinion Research Center, from the beginning of the 1990s, there has been a decline in the number of people considering the Beneš decrees (applying the collective guilt) as an act of justice. However, it is still a dominant way of perceiving the post-war events – in 2016, 37 % of Czech people viewed the Beneš decrees as fair, another 25 % considered them unfair but something

---

24 The topic of the Germans' post-war expulsion and their portrayal as *the others* was reflected in pop culture, especially in cinematography, which illustrates the changes in the perception of post-war events. The communist period filmmaking framed the topic of the German expulsion as a just act that was a legitimate way of dealing with war wrongdoings. However, in the post-1989 cinema, there are also motifs portraying the post-war deportations not only as an "act of justice" but also capturing the injustices of violence and murders committed by the Czechs (often motivated by property gain, not justice or vengeance).
25 This means that a process of reconciliation has occurred at the level of official interstate relations.
26 It is also worth mentioning the relatively strong "anti-Sudeten" groups within the Czech democratic left and right, which strongly protested against the adoption of the Czech-German convention.

that was a result of historical circumstances and should be put to rest. Only 9 % of the population think it is something that should be apologised for, and only 4 % claim that it is not enough to apologise and that the property must be returned and the rightful owners compensated (CVVM 2016, p. 1). When asked whether the Decrees should remain in effect, 43 % of people in 2016 spoke in favour, 45 % were unable to answer, and 12 % agreed with their annulment (CVVM 2016, p. 2). Considering this opinion pattern of Czech citizens (and therefore voters), it is evident that, when grasped appropriately, it can play an important political role.

As a matter of interest, we can illustrate the anti-German attitudes on the example of the current Czech President Miloš Zeman.[27] Throughout the whole development after the Velvet Revolution, it is possible to find several strong Zeman's statements against Germany, mainly regarding the Sudeten German question. Already in 1994, he stated it was inadmissible to consider the restitution of property confiscated after the war from the German residents and their return to the Czech Republic. He also criticised the forthcoming Czech-German declaration, whose goal was to terminate the history of mutual conflicts. Not long before the presidential election in 2003, he called the Sudeten Germans Hitler's fifth column, which was quite unfortunate considering the Czech efforts to join the EU. Among other things, it led to the postponement of German Chancellor Gerhard Schröder's visit. We can also see Miloš Zeman attacking specific individuals – for example, he compared the Sudetendeutsche Landsmannschaft leader (Sudeten German Homeland Association's leader) Bernd Posselt, based on his appearance, to 'Hitler after fattening'. In other cases, Zeman adopted historical references related to Sudeten Germans or Nazism for labelling people whom he viewed as his political opponents – he compared the Palestinian leader Yasser Arafat to Adolf Hitler, or above all, already in 1992, he compared the Federal Prime Minister Václav Klaus to the Sudeten Nazi Konrad Henlein with regard to the plan for the dissolution of Czechoslovakia, he denounced Klaus' effort to destroy the state as unconstitutional as were the Sudeten

---

27 For more information on Miloš Zeman's attitudes towards the Germans and Germany, see some works by Vladimír Naxera (2021a, 2021b). Some paragraphs of this text dedicated to Zeman's (and generally Czech historical) perception of Germans and Germany are based on these texts.

German efforts to dissolve the state before the Second World War (Kopeček 2017, passim).

Zeman presented the most interesting comments on the historical relation to Germany within the debates before the second round of the first direct presidential election in 2013. During this campaign, Zeman's opponent Karel Schwarzenberg[28] was repeatedly labelled a politician who defends the interests of the Sudeten Germans and whose motivation for being elected is the restitution of the confiscated German property. A whole range of false statements was produced within the campaign – for example, the one that the above-mentioned Bernd Posselt supported Schwarzenberg's candidacy. Mainly in the discussion broadcasted by the Czech Television, both candidates clashed over the issue of the Beneš decrees. In this exchange of views, Miloš Zeman played a role of a protector of the nation, whereas Schwarzenberg was forced into the position of someone from international circles trying to question the post-war deportation of the Germans. In the following discussion led across several media, many debating people (just like Zeman earlier) viewed Schwarzenberg as someone trying to disparage the post-war President Edvard Beneš and the patriotism of Czech soldiers and citizens and to jeopardise the property and ownership rights of the Czech citizens, by which he would de facto re-establish the Protectorate of Bohemia and Moravia (Jeřábek, Rösler & Sklenařík 2013, pp. 11–12).

Regarding the occupation and other conflicts (framed in the mythological structure by playing the role of myths of national catastrophe or trauma and myths of the Dark Age; cf. Košťálová 2012), it is necessary to mention two more actors whose historical influence is reflected in current politics. The first one is Russia. During the National Revival in the 19th century, many Pan-Slav revivalists kept their eyes on Russia. However, this trend

---

28 Karel Schwarzenberg (full name Karl Johannes Nepomuk Josef Norbert Friedrich Antonius Wratislaw Mena Fürst zu Schwarzenberg) is the member of the Czech branch of the German aristocratic Schwarzenberg family born in 1937. After the Communist coup in 1948, his family emigrated to Austrian exile. After the fall of the Communist régime, Schwarzenberg returned to his homeland. In 1990, he was appointed chancellor of the office of the president Václav Havel. Since these times, Schwarzenberg has been a member of the Czech political elite. In 2009, he established the new conservative party called TOP09. A significant part of his business companies is located in Austria.

declined and was replaced by the purely national concept of the Czech nation without emphasizing its affiliation to Slavic people.[29] The interwar Czechoslovakia maintained fair relations with the USSR. As most of the Czechoslovak territory was liberated by the Soviet army at the end of the war, the image of the USSR improved significantly in the Czech public discourse that deflected to the left as soon as the war was over. These introduced trends resulted in the establishment of the communist regime in 1948. In the 1960s, there comes a gradual liberalisation process known as the Prague Spring (Skilling 1970) that was ended in 1968 by the invasion of the armies of the Soviet Union and other members of the Warsaw Pact. The Soviet troops remained present after 1968 and stayed even until a couple of years after the fall of Communism. A Soviet soldier in the streets of the Czech cities became a symbol of *the others* or national enemies. In the post-Communist development, this occupation of more than 20 years became a part of political discourse as a negative historical experience.[30] It was expressed institutionally by the Czech Republic joining the Western structures, including NATO. For a large part of the society, anti-Russian positions are in fact related to anti-communist opinions (see Hrubeš & Navrátil 2017, 2018) and affected by the Russian attitude toward Central European countries, by their attempts to interfere with these countries' politics, by Russia's support for disinformation websites (e.g. Jarkovská 2020). Some anti-Russian attitudes of Czech society are also related to the fact that many ethnic Russians currently live in the Czech Republic, buying a considerable amount of real estate, mainly in Prague. Their economic

---

29 However, some (neo)Pan-Slavic currents appeared even during the First World War and after Czechoslovakia was declared. Among others, Karel Kramář, the first prime minister of the newly proclaimed state, was a supporter of the idea of a Slavic state under Russian leadership.
30 It is quite interesting that in 1945, in addition to Soviet troops, the Polish and Romanian units also took part in the liberation of Czechoslovakia from the east. However, after the war, the pro-Soviet sympathies erased the participation of other countries from the collective memory. On the contrary, when the Polish or Hungarian troops, for example, participated in the 1968 occupation, their behaviour was no better than that of the Soviets. Even so, it was the Soviets who have been blamed within the collective memory. The rest were somehow exculpated.

presence is often associated with their former military presence (Klvaňová 2019). However, in current Czech politics, we can also find strong pro-Russian attitudes that are often carried by the same subjects presenting the anti-German and anti-Muslim attitudes.

That brings us to the third historical experience with conflict and a threat of occupation and subjugation related to the efforts of the Ottoman Empire to invade Europe militarily. 'Turks at Vienna'[31] is a concept that has become a timeless metaphor for the Islamic danger to Europe and was revived mostly in relation to today's alleged immigration crisis. Although the Muslim community in the Czech Republic is insignificant in numbers and relatively well-integrated (Beránek & Ostřanský 2016), and almost no Muslims came to the Czech Republic as a part of the immigration wave of the last couple of years, Muslims have been put into the number one position of *the others*. It is a part of the trending European populism where Islam has become the main target of the *new xenophobia* (Khair 2016). In the Czech environment, the image of a 'Turk at Vienna' is often used as a timeless metaphor and evidence for Muslims' ancient aspiration to conquer Europe.

All the mentioned cases have something in common – although they originate in the past, they are reflected in current political affairs. If we looked at more potential *others* and historical enemies of the Czech politics, we would not find many, which is caused by the fact that for the most part of Modern history, the Czech lands belonged to the Habsburg Monarchy, they could not pursue their own policy, and thus do not have experience with other occupations (except those already mentioned). The Swedish presence in Prague during the Thirty Years' War was only episodic, and the reference to the 'Swedish in Prague' cannot serve the purposes of the process of othering. After establishing the new state in 1918, Czechoslovakia experienced two armed conflicts with Poland and Hungary; however, they are not really part of the collective memory. The last potential *others* might be the Slovaks. Although they occasionally appear in the nationalist discourse ('Slovak workers take the jobs from the Czechs'), however, considering the smooth dissolution of Czechoslovakia in 1992 (Bookman 1994), not even

---

31 This refers to two Turkish sieges of Vienna. Vienna was, in fact, the capital of the Habsburg Monarchy that also included the Czech lands. Especially the second Battle of Vienna in 1683 was one of the pivotal moments of European history.

the Slovaks serve unambiguously as *the others* in the sense of non-members, much less the enemies of the nation.

All of these *others* of the Czech politics mentioned above are essential for our research as well – as we will show in the section on studying the Liberation Festival in Pilsen, references to Germans, Muslims and Russians/Soviets as enemies are quite common in speeches delivered during the celebrations. However, there is one significant difference – with a few exceptions, the Germans are presented as a historical enemy but a current ally. That means there was a reconciliation (cf. Bar-Siman-Tov 2004), even though a large part of Czech society and political representation sees Germany as a problem (see above).

The three indicated groups of *the others* apply in a way to the example of Slovakia. Despite a partially different historical experience, the Slovaks encountered the German power (during the Second World War), the Russian/Soviet occupation after 1968, and the fight against the Turks, who occupied a large part of Hungary during their campaign in Europe. For that reason, we encounter various references to these three groups as part of the SNU celebrations in Banská Bystrica. In the relevant chapter, however, we will show that at least in some cases, this happens differently than during the Pilsen celebrations.

Nevertheless, in the Slovak case, it is necessary to mention two other important examples of *the others*. We will do so briefly and only for completeness because these two groups are not presented as problematic in the discourse connected with the festivities analysed in Banská Bystrica. The first group of *the others* are definitely Hungarians. The Slovak national revival of the 19th century occurred in entirely different conditions than in the case of the Czechs. We can consider Slovaks as a non-ruling ethnic group without historical statehood (cf. Hroch 1999; for the political context of building the identity of stateless nations, see also Zákravský 2017), although there are many attempts to incorporate the references to ancient state-like formations, mainly the Samo's Empire and Great Moravia, into Slovak history (e.g. Lupták 2008).[32] Thus, the modern Slovak nation was

---

32 As a matter of interest, let us add that the legacy of these two state units is often adopted also by the popularizing narratives on Czech history and identity. In practice, we see how the myth of beginning works (cf. Hroch 2009).

built in the conditions of the Kingdom of Hungary, facing the Hungarian political and cultural dominance[33] (cf. Křen 2005). The incorporation of the territory of today's Slovakia into the Hungarian state supports the still-living myth of the thousand-year oppression (as an exemplary "Dark Age"; see above), which is also reproduced by many political leaders:

> Slovaks did not have their own state for more than a thousand years. We were ruled by others, or we existed in a common state with others. There were times when the Slovak language was illegal, and our schools were closed; even in churches, it was not allowed to preach in Slovak. Despite this, we have preserved our language, as well as our culture, faith, and territory. Although we are a young state, we are also one of the oldest nations in this area. (Ivan Gašparovič, former president of the Slovak Republic; quoted in Lupták 2009, p. 155)

The historical legacy of Hungarian-Slovak relations affects, to a large extent, current relations (cf. Lupták 2009), although it must be said that this is not only a one-sided problem of Slovakia's relationship with Hungary (cf. Michela & Vöros 2013; Pitař 2012). The second example of *the others* is the Czechs. Although Slovaks had their first modern statehood within Czechoslovakia established in 1918, it needs to be mentioned that Czechoslovakia functioned primarily as an enlarged Czech state with a clear Czech political dominance. The Slovak nation's existence was not formally recognised and was overshadowed by the idea of "Czechoslovakism". Some elements of the Czech political representation's perspective on Slovakia de facto corresponded to the principles of Orientalism (cf. Said 1978). Internal disagreements resulted in the declaration of autonomy in the autumn of 1938 and eventually the Slovak state's independence in the spring of 1939 (we will return to the question of the Slovak state in the chapter on the SNU anniversary celebrations). It was in this period that the Czechs conclusively became *the others*[34] (cf. Lupták 2008).

What we discussed above – the issue of memory and history, their connection to creating national mythology and the often-derived images of

---

33 The fact that the higher socio-economic classes of Slovaks were assimilated into the Hungarian system and participated in its functioning does not really fit into the desired image of national mythology and is being ignored for the most part.

34 This can be illustrated, among other things, by the fact that in some cases there had been efforts to expel the Czechs from the Slovak territory even before that, that is, in the period of the Second Republic.

national friends, enemies, and *the others* – is part of what can best be described as soft memory. In order for this soft memory to perform (not only) the functions mentioned above, it needs to be connected to what Alexander Etkind (cf. 2004; 2013) refers to as hard memory and Pierre Nora (1989) as *Lieux de Mémoire*. It is necessary to "materialise" the memory and the remembering (and also forgetting) in the form of physical sites of memory, such as memorials, monuments, trauma sites, memory sites, sacral topography of cities, museums, and other objects, where it is possible to "touch the history" or relate it to a specific date in the political calendar (or both in the form of a public festivity commemorating a given historical event at a physical site of memory defined by this event). This is what we discuss in the next section.

Political calendars, holidays, commemoration, and *Lieux de Mémoire*

Political calendars play a crucial role in creating identity and consolidating collectivity. This is especially evident in cases of qualitative changes of regimes (cf. Hájková et al. 2018). In the case of Czechoslovakia, this happened several times during modern political history. Should it be with the establishment of Czechoslovakia, which introduced a number of new political holidays to build the identity in contrast to the existing Austria-Hungary (Čechurová 2018), above all the celebrations of the 28th October, the day the republic was established (Hájková & Michela 2018); with the advent of the communist regime, which introduced several new holidays; or finally, with the period after the fall of Communism (e.g. November 17 in the Czech Republic and Slovakia – this day refers to the beginning of demonstrations against the communist government) and the disintegration of the Czecho-Slovak state.

In all these cases, new holidays were created while some of the existing ones remained – their interpretation was modified to match the existing ideological framework. It can be May 1, celebrated before and after the establishment of Czechoslovakia (Horák 2018) but transformed after the arrival of the communist regime (Kubina 2014). Another category may be the holidays that continued to be celebrated in the same form, even though the regime had changed (e.g. Frýbertová 2014).[35] Some holidays have not transformed despite the political change – the already-mentioned October 28 is still celebrated as a national holiday of the Czech Republic, although it commemorates the state that no longer exists. To some extent, this also supports the fact mentioned earlier – after its establishment in 1918, Czechoslovakia was merely an enlarged Czech state. It can be seen on current holidays in the Slovak political calendar as well. The day October 28 is not one of them (this day is not classified as a national holiday but as a day of remembrance, which means it is not a bank holiday), and is replaced with two holidays connected with the establishment of the independent Slovak state – January 1 as the Day of the Establishment of the Slovak Republic, and September 1 as the Day of the Constitution of the Slovak Republic (the constitution was adopted on September 1, 1992, before the disintegration of the federation). The way the calendar of national holidays is politically constructed, de facto indicating what should be remembered (and ignoring what should be forgotten), is one of the primary instruments for hierarchizing the myths contained in national mythology (Mannová 2019, p. 51).

What events and personalities (when, where, and how) are politically remembered, commemorated, celebrated, forgotten, and ignored can be seen as an essential instrument for legitimizing the political regime (Benazzo 2017, p. 198), including the post-socialist regimes. Post-socialist societies have several specific features, not to mention the unique way they instrumentalise the past (see Staniszkis 1999). In these societies or regimes, distancing from the communist period became a political calculation aiming for rejuvenation and opposition against the past regime (by changing the political calendar and the sacralised topography of the city and landscape[36])

---

35 In the Slovak case, the same applies to the SNU anniversary which was celebrated immediately after the end of the war (e.g. Michela 2020a), during the communist regime (Michela 2020b) and after its fall, while the ideological framework changed considerably (Mannová 2008).
36 Which in some cases has been commercialised. For example, some of the removed statues celebrating the heroes of the communist regime in Budapest were moved outside the city to the "Statue Park" after the fall of the regime – a place that serves as one of the tourist attractions (Verdery 1999, p. 6).

(Benazzo 2017, p. 201)³⁷. In the way the post-communist regimes work with the (re)interpretation of the past regime, it is also typical for the political actors at public commemorations to link the commemorated event to the experience with Communism (even though there might be no association of the commemorated event/site with the communist regime whatsoever) (Tomczuk 2016, p. 108). The political construction of the calendar of national holidays and the physical sites of memory, and the incorporation of national mythology's elements into major constitutive texts and education curricula is a way of creating the nation's historicity and determining its significant (or almost essential) events and personalities (Abăseacă 2018, p. 672).

Historical legacy, whether in the form of a national holiday, special day, chapter in a textbook, or a depiction in a state symbol, is a tool connecting the past (preferably framed as "famous", "prosperous", etc.) with the present (Wittenberg 2015, p. 370). This link between the past and the present works better when the past is "reachable", when one can "feel its presence". This role is fulfilled by physical sites of memory (Munro 2020, p. 118), which are established from above (officially) or from below (unofficially) and very often have a strong emotional dimension (Moshenska 2020, p. 154). Sites of memory are thus places that are dedicated to the memory and have several interrelated meanings – from material and symbolic through functional and commemorative to political. Lieux de mémoire thus serves as an instrument for reminding important events and personalities and, thanks to the meaning contained in them, fulfils the abovementioned function of a link between the past and the future (cf. Nora 1989, 2010). Simply put, physical sites of memory can be seen as material representations of narratives about events and people who were/are important to a particular community to such an extent that they deserve a public spotlight (Cingerová & Dulebová 2020, p. 71). Therefore, memorial

---

37 This opposition can be amplified by the way in which the communist regime instrumentalised the creation of memorials. Memorials related to the conflict of the Second World War and its commemoration were framed by the regime in such way that the war was a fight with the Nazis who pursued capitalist and imperialist goals and whose efforts were thwarted by Communist-led people (Mannová 2019, p. 43).

spaces can strengthen the consensus (or conflict in the case of competing narratives) within society regarding the interpretation of the past (Tomczuk 2016, p. 105).

Memory places perform a series of functions. One of the most important is that they enable the localisation of memories; they serve as a symbolic bridge for crossing from the present to the past and back. At the same time, referring to these places (when appropriately instrumentalised) can be a source of political mobilisation – for example, in the form of "encouraging the present" by heroizing the deeds of those who are commemorated in the site of memory (cf. Forchtner 2016). From this point of view, the physical sites of memory – whether they are memorials, museums, monuments, trauma sites, reconciliation sites, graves, statues, or the names of locations in the sacralised topography of cities and landscapes – can be seen as a result of state apparatuses and power institutions trying to achieve the form of the past that they desire (D'Orsi 2015, p. 173).

On the one hand, the past left some traces on its own; on the other, references to the past are artificially (re)constructed in the form of graves, archives, museums, libraries, memorials, monuments,[38] or statues (Mannová 2019, p. 9). In this manner, the past is transferred to public space where it is relived and removed from temporality by being anchored in one specific place (D'Orsi 2015, p. 162). Speaking of the physical sites of memory, we can return to the apt metaphor of comparing the past to a supermarket since sites of memory have another strong dimension (although probably as an externality) – their commercial capacity. History and mythology sell well, so they are a convenient commodity (Mannová 2019, p. 11). Both in the form of a regular commodity (a souvenir with a "definitely authentic" piece of the Berlin Wall, a "liberty burger" at the Pilsen Liberation Festival, a plastic tank model bought at a stand next to the SNU museum during the annual celebrations), as well as in the form of a "political commodity" enabling the instrumentalisation of a celebrated event using the symbolism of a given site of memory (cf. Alexander 2006) to achieve political goals.

---

38 Regarding October 28 mentioned above, we can add that monuments commemorating the founding of the Czechoslovak state are among the most common monuments in the Czech setting (cf. Müller 2016).

In order to achieve the above, it is appropriate to produce a strong emotional appeal – use the lieux de mémoire to evoke strong feelings (pride, fear, sadness, nostalgia) (Mannová 2019, p. 27). It can be achieved by instrumentalizing trauma sites. These are a tool for transmitting, documenting and reifying traumatic events (Violi 2012, p. 43) and a tool that can bring cultural and social transformation (in the sense of a lesson learned and defining oneself; McLean 2010, p. 355) on one side but also political mobilisation and creation and strengthening of social cleavages on the other. One example of the use of trauma sites in the Czech context are the memorials in Lidice and Lety in the district of Písek. The Lidice Memorial is a trauma site commemorating the Nazi extermination of the village of Lidice in 1942 and thus represents a typical site of memory that fulfils the commemorative functions. At the same time, it allows the connection of the physical site of memory with the category of *the others* (Germans). This is one of the reasons why Lidice are often the centre of activities of the nationalist groups, for which the Germans still represent the enemy. These groups do not accept the reconciliation that was made at the official level.

A similar function of a trauma site is represented by the Lety Memorial commemorating the labour camp for Roma established during the Second World War. The Roma have long sought (through various cultural institutions and political actors) public recognition of the camp's existence and creating a dignified site of memory related to this trauma site. A piggery grew on the site of this former labour camp, and the discussion about its demolition and replacement with a trauma site has long been causing a political and social cleavage, which manifested in some right-wing extremist politicians calling the camp a "non-existent pseudo concentration camp".[39]

---

39 However, questioning the Roma holocaust is not a domain of the far-right. We find similar attitudes also in democratic left-wing and right-wing groups as well as in the communists. After all, the Czech communists do not fulfil the presumed idea of internationalism in any way – they are (and to a large extent, were before 1989) a strongly nationalist party. From the beginning of the 1990s, they have been resolutely opposing the German claims (real or imagined) to return to the Sudetenland, parts of which were long one of the electoral strongholds of the Communist Party (throughout the 1990s and even after the beginning of the new millennium).

However, this dispute once again confirmed the image of *the others* – the Roma, in this case (cf. Kailemia 2016) (who, according to one narrative, wanted to demolish a prosperous piggery and replace it with a memorial). The two memorials are connected by what Katherine Verdery calls the politics of dead bodies – the fact that dead bodies are a strong source of political mobilisation and political conflict (Verdery 1999, p. 36).

The camp in Lety and the discussions around it indicate that places of physical memory tend to have considerable conflict potential resulting from the connection of different ideological frameworks with the celebrated (or condemned) past. Let us move from the examples of the post-socialist political necromancy at the trauma sites in Lidice and Lety to the illustration of the conflict and mobilisation potential of the "bronze corpse" (sculpture) represented by the removal of a prominent person from temporality and their "immortalisation" (Verdery 1999, p. 5). We can look at other examples from the Czech and Slovak context; in the Czech case, a good illustration of disputes over statues can be found in discussions about removing the statue of Soviet Marshal Ivan Stepanovich Konev. The figure of Konev is represented by several lines – during the Second World War, he commanded the Eastern Front troops, which drove the Germans out of much of Central and Eastern Europe and took part in the conquest of Berlin. After the war, he remained in prominent positions; however, he took part in events that in many ways overshadowed his share in the defeat of the Germans. These included the bloody suppression of the Hungarian uprising in 1956, the construction of the Berlin Wall, or his controversial share in the occupation of Czechoslovakia in 1968. Konev's statue was erected in Prague in 1980, officially on the occasion of the 35th anniversary of the liberation of Czechoslovakia. Disputes over the statue began shortly after the fall of the communist regime when several other statues reminiscent of the earlier regime were removed.

However, the final decision was made by the dominant right-wing council of the given city district in 2019. The statue was finally removed in the spring of 2020 after it had been damaged repeatedly. For several days, the news was filled with clashes between opponents and supporters of the removal. Proponents of the statue's removal mainly argued that the statue is not a reminder of Prague's liberation by the Red Army, such as a monument to fallen soldiers built immediately after the war would be, but a manifestation of Soviet imperialism and symbolic consolidation of Soviet power over Czechoslovakia that, by the time of the statue's construction, the Soviet troops had occupied for more than ten years. On the side of the removal's opponents, a diverse range of politicians joined forces, from Communists to the far-right – political currents that have long rejected the Czech Republic's pro-Western orientation and turned to cooperation with Russia (or China). The removal of the statue resulted, among other things, in criminal prosecution initiated by the Russian Federation. The country has a law of up to five years in prison for destroying war graves or monuments, both in Russia and abroad. The chapter on the Pilsen celebrations will later return to the debate regarding the perception of the relationship with the USSR and Russia.[40]

A dispute over statues from the Slovak context can be illustrated with the background of the unveiling of the statue of the prophets Cyril and Methodius,[41]

---

40 Regarding the removal of the Konev's statue, it is not without interest that at a similar time in one of Prague's city districts the council (consisting of similar right-wing forces as the council that decided to remove Konev's monument) decided to build a monument dedicated to the Vlasovs (Russian Liberation Army). These Russian troops under General Andrey Andreyevich Vlasov that fought (for various reasons) against the USSR during the war also had their share in the Prague uprising, which preceded the liberation of Prague by the Red Army. Fights against Soviet troops brought not only the end of the Vlasovs after they fell into Soviet captivity, but also the ideology-based reflection of the Russian Liberation Army within the communist historiography. The fact that at the same time similarly politically oriented local governments of two different Prague districts are simultaneously demolishing a statue of a Soviet marshal and erecting a monument to other Russian troops shows how much these anti-Russian attitudes are influenced by anti-communism and defining oneself against Soviet/Russian imperialism (real or imagined).

41 Cyril and Methodius are heralds of faith who, on behalf of the rulers of Great Moravia, brought Christianity from the Byzantine Empire to this early feudal Slavic state. In the Czech Republic and Slovakia, July 5, associated with Cyril and Methodius, is a national holiday. This also shows the already indicated creation of a connection (albeit highly ahistorical) between Great Moravia and the current state of Czechs and Slovaks. Within the Slovak national mythology, however, both heralds have a stronger position than in the case of contemporary Czech mythology. This influence is evident not only in the number of statues of the heralds throughout Slovakia (one of them is in Banská Bystrica, the place

which was erected[42] in the summer of 2010 at a newly built roundabout in Komárno.[43] For several years, there have been disputes over the location of the statue. In 2003, Matica slovenská failed to negotiate with the city management the location of a new sculpture in one of the historic squares, so eventually, it was installed on the facade of the local House of Matica Slovenská. However, the installation was performed without a building permit, so administrative proceedings began to be conducted against the construction. Before the 2010 elections, Prime Minister Robert Fico agreed with Matica slovenská on relocating the sculpture to a new busy roundabout (although the local society of Matica was against it). Fico described the statue, which was protested by a part of the public and which, according to the then-Mayor of Komárno Tibor Bastrnák, was again installed without a building permit, as a "gift to the citizens of the city". The statue was ceremoniously unveiled in the presence of Prime Minister Robert Fico (shortly before the end of his term), prominent politicians from Fico's party, and other VIP guests. The whole event, which lasted about an hour, was organised by a private company contracted by the Office of the Government.[44]

A conflict was caused already by the discussions on whether the statue should be installed or not. From our perspective, it was also interesting that the very act of the statue's erection did not go without conflicts. Leaving

---

of our research of many years) but also in the fact that before the adoption of the Euro, the pair was depicted on one of the Slovak banknotes. However, Cyril and Methodius also belong to the entire European Christian tradition and are co-patrons of Europe.

42 We attended the ceremonial unveiling of the statue and the notes below are based on our field research (see also Krčál & Naxera 2011). We already mentioned this in the Prologue.

43 Komárno was originally a historic Hungarian town on the southern border of Slovakia. After the establishment of Czechoslovakia in 1918, there was a conflict with Hungary, which did not want to give up the city. The Hungarian effort was unsuccessful and only a smaller suburb south of the border river Danube remained part of the Hungarian territory. At present, Hungarians make up more than 50 % of the city's population.

44 It can be assumed that the event was originally planned as a ceremonial confirmation of Fico's election victory and with a motive of following the Komárno tradition of statues construction alternating between the Slovaks and Hungarians. However, due to the election results, this dimension was somewhat weakened.

aside a small number of attendees who protested mainly against Robert Fico and his party, as well as the majority of the audience actively supporting the event,[45] what was particularly interesting was the participation of Hungarian nationalists. These attendees brought Hungarian flags, flags of the Sixty-Four Counties Youth Movement (aiming to unite all Hungarians into one state), and Hungarian-Slovak banners with messages such as "We welcome the Slovak tourists in our city of Komárno". The group also tried to disrupt the speeches of the elites by playing music, chanting, and whistling. Every time Robert Fico's name was mentioned, they ran a siren into the megaphone, not turning it off at all during Fico's speech.[46]

As the above suggests, memory places represent a relevant field of political rivalry when trying to promote the desired interpretation of the past. This is most evident when the political order changes qualitatively. At times of a radical regime change, there are, of course, significant changes in sites of memory – transformations of dead bodies carved in stone and cast in bronze that represent certain values and ideals (Verdery 1999, p. 6). Within political necromancy, they are removed, torn down and possibly replaced by other (more suitable) places where one can "touch the past".

---

45 It was interesting that many Slovak flags were raised in the audience during the whole event. After, however, no one took it home; they were all handed over to the organizers in the back area. Therefore, the expressions of sympathy were not spontaneous, but were organised and can be understood as part of the whole performance (cf. Goffman 1966).

46 Komárno is similarly interesting when it comes to other controversies regarding the construction of the statues. In the summer of 2009, Hungarian President László Sólyom planned to visit Komárno in order to pay a visit to the construction of the statue of Saint Stephen, the first king of Hungary. The unveiling of the statue was organised mostly by the Hungarians and was under the auspices of the mayor. The unveiling as well as the visit were scheduled for August 21. On this day in 1968, the occupation of Czechoslovakia by the Warsaw Pact troops (including Hungarian troops) began. Also, for this reason, a number of Slovak politicians called the President's visit a provocation. Among other things, it was because the president did not intend to meet with his Slovak counterpart, or the prime minister or the Speaker of the Parliament. The three of these highest Slovak constitutional officials later declared that Sólyom was not a "welcome guest", and he was in a very curious way "forbidden" to enter the country. In the end, Sólyom reached only the middle of the bridge over the border River Danube, where he held a press conference (for more, see Lupták 2010:156–157).

There are numerous fitting examples of that in the demolition of statues of Soviet leaders throughout Central and Eastern Europe at the turn of the 1980s and 1990s, as well as the removal of Soviet tanks or fighter jets that stood on many memorial squares and village squares of (not only) Czech and Slovak towns and villages. This proves that sites of memory are always a reification of power institutions' symbolic dominance that usurp public space and use it for their own purposes (Mannová 2019, p. 306). On their part, the sites of memory are always given a new meaning just at the moment when there are fundamental changes in the political and social context (Mannová 2019, p. 283). What was appropriate and desired in the past (from the previous regime's perspective) is now inappropriate and undesirable (cf. McLean 2010).

In addition to dealing with sites of memory and most often with bronze and stone dead bodies, another way of coping with the inappropriate past is a change in the sacralised topography of the city and landscape. In this regard, it is natural that the names of important landscape or urban elements (streets, boulevards, squares) represent an important subject expressing ideological-political dominance (cf. Sereda 2012). If we return to the Czechoslovak context, we can say that the political creation of sacralised topography is one of the tools by which Czechoslovaks (and later Czechs and Slovaks) defined themselves against the unsuitable past. The names of streets, squares, or entire cities were changed after the fall of the Habsburg Monarchy, after the Second World War, and after 1989, when the names were modified to the greatest extent – the names of the representatives of the labour and communist movement disappeared (Mannová 2019, p. 267), and one city was renamed; Gottwaldov – named after communist president Klement Gottwald – (again) became Zlín.

The extent to which physical sites of memory will be able to perform the above functions is greatly affected by their commemorative capacity – that is, the extent to which the given physical sites of memory (from memorials, statues and monuments through the names of streets, squares and hills to museums, libraries and archives) can successfully evoke in society a feeling of commemoration and thus bring a feeling of bridging the past and present. The specific format of the commemorative rituals is also important; how festivities and public political events are held, and what atmosphere can be created with these spectacular celebrations of the past (Tomczuk

2016, p. 108). This brings us to the last dimension of the "materialised past" – its public celebration.

Some physical sites of memory are invisible[47] for most of the year, given that they are an integral part of the urban environment. We walk past them daily, they serve as meeting points,[48] places of relaxation, but for most of the year, we ignore their original purpose; it reveals itself on the date that is set for it in the political calendar and the symbolism of time, place and event are brought together (cf. Alexander 2006). As a result, largely invisible places are suddenly the centre of attention of politicians, the media, and indirectly also the public (Mannová 2019, p. 309). In the context of public political events and related political festivities, sites of memory come to life, and it is in these moments that they are most often instrumentalised by participating political actors who use them as tools to legitimise their own political demands and (re)produce national and political identities (Tomczuk 2016, p. 109). These political rituals are thus a tool for transmitting, concretizing and reifying national myths (Mannová 2019, p. 60). Public political events in the form of ritualised celebrations/commemorations/remembrances are one of the key tools by which national mythology is recalled, maintained and modified, and which serve as a platform where collective identity is asserted inwards and, in some cases, outwards in the form of the image of *the others* that is being constructed and reminded.

The events that we examine and interpret and their annual commemorations fulfil the features mentioned above and can be perceived as a celebration of a historical turning point. Both the celebrations of the liberation of Pilsen in the form of the Liberation Festival and the Slovak National Uprising celebrations connect two historical periods and represent a transition between the "Dark Age" and the "renewal period", a divide

---

47 Not in the sense that they would not be "seen", but in the sense that we perceive them as a routine and ordinary part of the urban/landscape environment, and their initial functions are "visible" on clearly defined occasions.
48 Among other thing, the common phrase in Pilsen is "let's meet at the memorial", which frequently serves as a meeting point. This memorial is a monument called "Thank You, America!", which is located on Americká Avenue and connected with part of the celebrations. We will return to the memorial and the street in more detail in the related section.

between the unwanted and forced past caused externally by *the other* and the desired present (cf. Wittenberg 2015).

***

On the pages above, we outlined several theoretical and conceptual starting points of our research. We consider the most important of these to be national mythology, the concepts of *the others*, political calendars, sites of memory, and public festivities, which serve to commemorate the given past events' legacy.

In our research, all these concepts are interconnected. We focus on events during which there is an overlap of a significant date in the political calendar and a place of collective memory where a festivity is held commemorating that particular date. Such a date is usually linked to an important point in national mythology and serves, among other things, to negotiate who is/was or is not/was not a national enemy. This link is clearly evident both in the case of the Liberation Festival and in the case of the annual SNU anniversary celebrations. It is interesting to note that the enemies are not only those who were the architects of the "Dark Age" or "national oppression" followed by the liberation, but also those who represent *the others* in the current political and social discourse.

As we have illustrated, it is the post-socialist environment that is typical for the instrumentalisation of the past legacy as a way of supporting current political claims and vision of the future, which is in no way related to the commemorated history. Trauma sites, "dead bodies" (whether real or bronze) and sites of memory are used by the political representation strictly in line with the prevailing ideological framework. In particular, dead bodies (in the form of constant references to fallen warriors, most often with something like "they sacrificed themselves so that we could…") run through our research as well. Referring to the need to "act in such a way" so that our ancestors did not "die in vain" is a regular part of the commemorations in Pilsen and Banská Bystrica. This manner of using the historical legacy with an emphasis on human victims is one of the main subjects of our interest, and, inspired by the work of Katherin Verdery (1999), we call it "(post-socialist) political necromancy". Dead bodies are revived by politicians de facto playing the roles of necromancers. The revived bodies serve as an "army of the dead" to achieve political goals (whatever they may be).

Chapter 2 Liberation Festival in the most "American city" in Europe

The Liberation Festival is a several-day celebration and a commemoration of the liberation of Pilsen by American and Belgian troops at the end of the Second World War. Every year, the festivities follow a similar scenario and consist of a whole range of events – from official memorials through concerts to an accompanying programme for military enthusiasts. Pilsen was the largest Czech city that was not liberated by the Red Army, which affected the (non)celebration of liberation both before and after the fall of the communist regime. The Pilsen festival is one of the largest events associated with the celebrations of the U.S. Army in the entire Europe. From this perspective, only a few events can compete with it, including the commemoration event in Bastogne, Belgium. While in the case of Bastogne, there were hard and long battles, which are presented today in the Second World War museum located in this city, the liberation of Pilsen was relatively peaceful in comparison. Laconically speaking, it was almost without a shot. The massiveness of the Pilsen commemoration event, which has been held since the 1990s, is related to the defining against the communist past[49] and with a bit of exaggeration, it is a manifestation of the attitude described as "we were not able to celebrate it for years, so now we will celebrate in a big way". Concerning the change of regime and the mythology it was building, the tendency to celebrate the United States can also be seen as a foreign policy orientation after 1989 (and its symbolic annual validation). This turn from the USSR/Russia and inclination towards Europe and the transatlantic alliance – a metaphorical change of course from East to West after the Velvet Revolution – represents an effort to identify new pillars on which foreign policy, as well as society as a whole, will be able to

---

49 After all, the conservative right-wing Civic Democratic Party, which has governed in Pilsen most of the time since the fall of Communism to the present, is characterised by loudly articulated anti-communist positions, often linked to anti-Russian positions. We discussed this in the previous section in connection with the monuments to Marshal Konev and the Vlasovs.

rely in the period after the qualitative change of regime (see Hájková et al. 2018; cf. Havelka 2001).

In this section, we will introduce several interrelated topics that will guide the readers through our research of the festival. First, we will briefly present the celebrated event itself and the history of (non)celebration associated with the dominant ideology before 1989. Then we will focus on how the legacy of the liberation affected the map of the city of Pilsen and the entire cultural environment of Pilsen. We will introduce the course of the festivities and focus more deeply on analyzing the dominant discourses associated with the celebrations, especially in relation to negotiating positions towards *the others* and using historical references for supporting current political demands. Some ideas of this chapter have been published before (cf. Krčál & Naxera 2015, 2016, 2019; Naxera & Krčál 2019) – but now, the topic has been newly grasped, framed and interpreted from a different perspective based on the objective of the entire book.

Liberation of Pilsen and Western Bohemia

> In the morning hours of the 6th of June, 1944, Allied troops launched an attack on Wehrmacht units by landing in Normandy. D-Day, the day the Battle of Normandy began, became one of the most important events of the Second World War. A moment of surprise, determination and bravery of the soldiers succeeded, the liberation of the European continent began and lasted until May 1945. Some of the troops fighting on the beaches of Normandy reached Pilsen on their way to victory. […] The city of Pilsen, thanks to one of the most important historical events of the last century, the end of the Second World War, which fundamentally affected the fate of the people of Europe, found itself in a unique position. As one of the cities liberated in May 1945, it is the last real and symbolic place where the journey of the Allied troops through the European continent ended. A city that symbolically connects France, Luxembourg, Belgium, and the Czech Republic.

The quote is taken from the official website of the Liberation Festival (2020)

The beginning of Western Bohemia's liberation at the end of the Second World War can be dated to the fights in the Bavarian Forest (Český les) and the Bohemian Forest (Šumava) that broke out in the second half of April 1945. About two to three weeks later, specifically on May 7, American troops entered Pilsen that became part of modern national mythology as the main venue for festivities commemorating and adoring the U.S. military and its role during the Second World War. On the same day, the American troops also reached the town of Rokycany, located on the demarcation line (cf. Mucha 2009; Lehnerová 2017).

The involvement of the ground troops was preceded by air operations that began a year before the end of the war. At the end of 1944, Allied forces began bombing the Škoda Works plant in Pilsen (at that time, an important pillar of the arms industry of Nazi Germany). During October and then December, several bombing raids were repeated, the strongest one on December 20, claiming hundreds of casualties (not only among the Škoda factory workers but also as part of the collateral damage caused by bombs hitting residential houses). The aerial operations preceding the infantry invasion culminated in April 1945 with three strong air raids (the effectiveness of which was amplified by weak resistance from the Germans). The first wave came on the night of the 16th and 17th, when the Burgher Brewery and the adjacent workers' colony were hit by mistake instead of the Škoda factory. The bombing claimed more than 600 civilian casualties. The second wave of the bombing came a day later. On April 17, the Allied bombers aimed for the Škoda Works again, but due to heavy flak, they were forced to drop the bombs before reaching the target, striking an entirely residential part of Pilsen. The last wave of April 25 was the most effective regarding the plan to incapacitate the Škoda Works plant, and after this raid, the production of this industrial complex was completely paralysed (Plzeň 1945 2018).

However, within the mythological structure of the myth of freedom, the liberation of Pilsen cannot be seen only as freedom guaranteed externally by American and Belgian troops (although it is the dominant narrative). The reason for this is the fact that as a result of the Prague uprising (of the May 5), the revolutionary spirit spread to Pilsen, and the Pilsen uprising began on the same day (which is being remembered in the narrative structure of the Liberation Festival, but not with the same importance as the liberation from the outside). As part of the Pilsen uprising, German flags were torn down, German inscriptions were rewritten and replaced with Czech equivalents. German soldiers were attacked, and the city's occupation authorities were imprisoned. The most important move of the Pilsen uprising was taking control of the radio transmitter that served the rebels as a tool for communication and for disinforming the Nazi troops. The uprising could have ended in bloodshed, as the commander-in-chief of German troops in the area had several thousand men at his disposal, and the rebels (with a few exceptions and participating police officers) had no heavy weapons to use. Negotiations between these actors eventually led to the German troops retreating, provided that the rebels would return the seized equipment and the German civilians would be free to leave the city (Plzeň 1945 2018). Nonetheless, the Pilsen uprising was not without casualties; at the 2016 Liberation Festival, a new site of memory was dedicated to the commemoration of the killed participants – a memorial to the fallen people of Pilsen. Memorial events at this site have become an integral part of celebrations' dramaturgy (see Kriegerová 2016).

The entrance of Allied troops into Pilsen itself was relatively smooth and without significant resistance; the soldiers were welcomed by the people of the city. The turning point came when the troops arrived in the central square of Pilsen, where the German soldiers opened fire from several houses and the church tower in the last act of resistance. The liberation of Pilsen can be considered complete with the commander of German troops in the city von Majewski surrendering to the Allied forces (and subsequently committing suicide) (Plzeň 1945 2018; for detailed photo documentation of the liberation of Western Bohemia, cf. Roučka 2005).

History of (non)celebration and sites of collective memory

Although the celebrations of the American liberation of Pilsen were held immediately in the post-war years, the tradition was quickly renounced after the communist coup in 1948. In the official narratives of communist Czechoslovakia, the American role in liberating the country was neglected, and all credit was given to the Red Army. It was not just the case of Pilsen – the demarcation line that, according to the agreement among the Allies, separated the American and Soviet zones ran northeast from Pilsen and passed through the town of Rokycany, which was liberated by the American as well as Soviet armies. After the war, there was a monument in the city commemorating these events, and celebrations were dedicated to both armies (cf. Lehnerová 2017). However, after the arrival of the communist regime, all remarks of the American participation were removed from the public space, new places of collective memory were established (such as the Red Army soldier statue, which is now in a nearby museum dedicated to the demarcation line), and only the Soviet part continued to be celebrated.

The situation with the Pilsen celebrations was very similar. There were also several different versions of "historical truth" – not just that the Red Army liberated the city, but also that the city was liberated by Red Army soldiers disguised in American uniforms. If the American presence in the region was mentioned, it was with negative connotations. In 1953, for example, the publication *Americans in Western Bohemia* (Bartošák & Pichlík 1953) came out, presenting the American activities as imperialist, criminal, and de facto terrorist.

One of the motifs of how the American activities were being recalled was the already mentioned bombing of the Škoda factory in Pilsen, one of the key arms factories of the Third Reich. Therefore, it is not surprising that at the end of the war, it was one of the most bombed places in the Protectorate. The bombing affected not only the adjacent districts but Pilsen as such. In a number of old city quarters situated around the factory or the railway station, there are still gaps between the old apartment buildings where the houses were struck during the bombing. The bombing has become an integral part of some of the war narratives of the people of Pilsen.[50]

---

50 This is illustrated with the memories of one of the authors: My grandmother comes from a family associated with the Škoda Works. Her father worked in the Škoda factory during the war. As told by her, during one of the air raids, he thoughtlessly grabbed the wooden workshop stool on which he had been sitting, and ran away from the factory through the sewer. After the raid, he realised that he had still been holding the stool in his hand. To this day, we have that stool at our cottage, and we sit on it by the fire (Vladimír).

Although the role of the factory was crucial, the later communist interpretation condemned the bombing, in particular, the devastating raid of April 1945, which was commonly described as senseless (a period propaganda quote taken from Toušek et al. 2014, p. 50):

> From the perspective of affecting the further course of the war and its results, this air raid made no sense at all. Its main goal was to make the post-war reconstruction of Czechoslovakia more difficult, making it economically more dependent on capitalist states.

The already-mentioned publication by Bartošák and Pichlík (1953) also deals extensively with the bombing of the Škoda Works:

> It was only over the little dead bodies of their children killed by American bombs that they understood. Only standing in front of the burning ruins of their houses did they realise that the American planes had brought death and destruction, blood and tears. [...] On the 17th and 18th of April 1945, three weeks before the end of the war, the American imperialists ordered their air forces to destroy and murder even in Pilsen. The raid of the 17th of April itself almost destroyed Škvrňany and Karlov, the working-class districts of Pilsen. The American bombs killed 624 citizens and injured 453. [...] That was not enough for the American barbarians. The very next day, they flew to Pilsen again, and again their planes sowed death. A total of 769 lives of Czech people in Pilsen fell victim to the American air raids of April 1945, and 542 people were injured. Five hundred five buildings were demolished and over 5,000 damaged. These were two-thirds of the houses in Pilsen. The American airstrikes took over seven and a half thousand apartments, depriving their inhabitants of shelter. The marshalling yard was destroyed, and Pilsen lost its slaughterhouse and the entire slaughter district. [...] On the 25th of April 1945, a large union of American bombers took off from a large military airport in North Africa, built during the war south of the city of Tunis. The order was brief: Destination – Pilsen in Western Bohemia. The mission – to destroy the largest factory of heavy engineering in the Czechoslovak Republic and the largest arms factory in Europe – Škoda Works.

In the following sections, the authors mention clear political and economic motives that led the "American imperialists" to bomb the factory:

> The American imperialists bombed Škoda because they wanted to destroy the industry that our working people were to take over and that were to serve the people. Because they wanted to eliminate any competition to their monopolies and heavy industry trusts. For these greedy goals of Wall Street, the American financial magnates did not hesitate for a moment to issue an order to destroy Škoda. They did not hesitate for a moment to kill hundreds of men and women

in Pilsen. To fill the pockets of the New York brokers, American planes scattered death in Pilsen.⁵¹

Finally, they did not avoid comparing the activities of Soviet and American troops on Czech territory. Below, we come to the conclusion that this interpretation is not so different from the current interpretation that, however, swaps the "sides of good and evil":

> Two armies came to Czechoslovakia in 1945. One from the East as the liberator of our nation from fascism, the other army, American, an enemy army to our people's democratic republic, with the orders of its Wall Street overlords – to disrupt political and economic life in the Czechoslovak Republic.

Therefore, according to the communist interpretation, American activities in Western Bohemia in 1945 were an obvious part of the wartime "Dark Age" era. The Red Army tanks then relieved Czechoslovakia of not only German but also American danger, which was necessary for starting a journey to national renewal and the Golden Age, culminating in the communist putsch in 1948. From this perspective, the Germans and Americans are enemies of Czechoslovakia – one defeated and "punished", the other still to watch out for. In this respect, these post-war processes of designating friends and enemies took place, to a greater or lesser extent, in large part of (Middle Eastern) Europe (e.g. Judt 2006).

After the fall of the communist regime, the framing of the Pilsen liberation changed immediately, and in May 1990, the first Liberation Festival took place. On the occasion of these 1990 celebrations, Jan Vyčítal wrote the song "It was that time in forty-five (when Patton liberated Pilsen)",

---

51 One interesting parallel can be mentioned here. While the communist propaganda criticised the bombing of the Škoda plants before the end of the war, the Soviet air force bombed other parts of the Czechoslovak territory shortly after the end of the war. One of the major raids took place on May 9, already after the German surrender, in Mladá Boleslav. German troops began to move to fall into American and not Soviet captivity. The Soviet air force under Marshal Konev carried out a massive raid, which resulted in death of about one hundred and fifty Czech civilians, the destruction of several dozen houses, and the damage to the railway station and the Mladá Boleslav car factory. This episode is interesting, among other things, in relation to the above-mentioned removal of the statue of Konev in 2020. This bombing was mentioned as one of the arguments why this statue should not stand in Prague.

which was first sung and recorded live during the festival and soon became one of the most played songs on Czech radio stations. Since 1990, the festival has been taking place every May, with the exception of 2020, when it was cancelled due to the COVID-19 pandemic and replaced with only a few online events. The celebrations' ideological framing has been more or less the same from the beginning (we will get to it below). The celebrations gradually turned into an extensive festival of several days, consisting of many various events.

From the very beginning, the festival focused on "liberation from the outside". Every year, the American presence at the festival is crucial. Dozens of American veterans participated already in the spontaneous celebrations in 1990. The largest number of them arrived in 1995 on the occasion of the 50th anniversary of the liberation – almost 200. Also, in 1995, one of the important sites of memory in the city of Pilsen was established – the "Thank you, America!" monument.

Emphasizing the alliance with the USA and celebrating and commemorating their role at the end of the war is omnipresent in Pilsen. This is reflected, among other things, in the number of places of physical memory with monuments and memorials, of which there are several dozen in Pilsen and the surrounding area and which have become privileged places of Pilsen city memory (Burzová et al. 2013). This emphasis also resonates in the sacralised topography of the city of Pilsen. There are obvious references to the role and importance of the United States – for example, one of the bridges on the central thoroughfare connecting the northern and southern parts of the city is called "Patton's Bridge"; the street, on which the "Thank you, America!" monument is located, is called Americká (American) Avenue.

The hardship associated with the monument's construction can briefly illustrate the above-indicated conflict and ideological burden of this topic. The history of the monument paying tribute to the U.S. military began almost immediately after the war. In 1946, an art competition was held, which brought the design for the monument. In the same year, the monument's foundation stone was laid. In 1948, after the communist coup, demonstrations were held at this place, and the members of the state police tried to prevent the people of the city from laying flowers and American flags at the foundation stone. The night after the protests, all the flowers, flags, and the stone itself were transported to a landfill; until the fall of the communist regime, the monument was not built. The foundation stone was re-laid in 1990 when the street was already named Americká, and in 1995, it was ceremoniously unveiled (cf. Paměť národa n.d.). Since then, the monument has served as a meeting point for the people of Pilsen, mainly thanks to its location in the city centre at the interchange of several public transport lines.

Even the monument's location is characterised by the fact that there were efforts to usurp it symbolically in the city's sacralised topography. The imprint that power institutions have on the names of locations of the city's public space and the changes in these names related to transformations of political and social context (cf. Mannová 2019, p. 283) can be illustrated with the genesis of naming the street that is today known as Americká Avenue and at the end of which stands the monument presented above (to which we will return further in the text). This street was initially named Stodolní (Barn Street), which referred to the barns located on its side. In 1873, it was renamed Jungmannova (Jungmann) Avenue.[52] After 1913, the street was extended thanks to a bridge[53] constructed over the river that had been dividing this street into two, until this time, unconnected units. The lower part of the street from the bridge to the railway station was called třída Františka Josefa I (Franz Joseph I Avenue) until 1918, when it was renamed Wilsonova (Wilson) Avenue. In 1940, when the reference to the American president was replaced with reference to a monarch, the street was named třída Karla IV (Charles IV Avenue). The upper part (Jungmannova Avenue) resisted the ideological renaming until 1941 when it was named třída Vítězství (Victory Avenue). After 1945, the lower part of the street was renamed back to Wilsonova Avenue, and the upper part was called Stalinova (Stalin) Avenue. In 1951, Stalin metaphorically

---

52 Josef Jungmann was a Czech philologist, writer and translator during the National Revival in the 19th century.
53 This bridge and how it was repeatedly renamed can illustrate the interventions of power institutions in the topography of the city. From the Bridge of Emperor Franz Joseph I, Wilson's Bridge, Bridge of Charles IV, Stalin's Bridge, and the Victory Bridge, it finally came back to Wilson's Bridge (Encyklopedie Plzeň 2019b). The name reflected the Austro-Hungarian era, then the era of interwar Czechoslovakia, a state that owed its formation, among others, to the U.S. President Wilson, the Communist era, and so on.

pushed Wilson out, and the entire street was connected and given a single name – Stalinova Avenue. Naturally, the power institutions in Pilsen also responded to later domestic political changes in the Soviet leadership and to the deconstruction of Stalin's cult (albeit with considerable delay and caution), and in 1962 "Stalin left Pilsen", and the street was renamed Moskevská (Moscow) Avenue. This title lasted[54] until the street was given its (so far) final name of Americká in 1991 (Encyklopedie Plzeň 2019a).

In Pilsen, however, there are several other memory sites associated with the American legacy. It is not only about dozens of small monuments and memorial plaques scattered throughout the city but also about a relatively new sculpture commemorating General Patton, who commanded the American troops liberating Pilsen. The unveiling of this monument in the presence of Patton's grandson was one of the central events of the 2015 festival. Additionally, there is a museum in Pilsen dedicated to the liberation, also bearing the name referring to the American general – Patton Memorial.

Apart from physical places of collective memory, Pilsen and America's symbolic connection is evident in many other aspects. During the festival, numerous speakers regularly mention that Pilsen is "the most American city in Europe". In recent years, American Street Food Festivals organised, among others, on the occasion of the Liberation Festival, have a strong tradition in Pilsen. The Pilsen brewery also regularly brews a special batch of American hop beer at this time. However, the most visible symbolic connection can be found in the case of the Pilsen ice hockey club, which began using a new logo in 2009 – the head of an Indian styled to resemble the patches of the Second American Infantry Division, which liberated Pilsen (see Fig. 1).

Festival's organisation and the course of celebrations

The Liberation Festival in Pilsen is an annual festivity, which in a ritualised form celebrates and commemorates the city's liberation by Allied troops at the end of the Second World War. It is a multi-day festival consisting of a wide range of events – from memorial events and commemorations through

---

54 With a short intermission, when the street bore the name Ludvík Svoboda Avenue, after the Czechoslovak president, for two years (1968–1970).

Fig. 1: *The patch of the Second Infantry Division that participated in liberating Pilsen (left) and the Pilsen ice hockey club logo introduced in 2009 (right)*

cultural and educational programmes to the (most attractive to viewers) stationary and dynamic demonstrations of the Second World War and contemporary military technology – taking place in various parts of Pilsen (and surrounding area). The thematic link connecting these events is the celebration of Pilsen's liberation by Allied (American and Belgian) troops.

A considerable number of viewers attend this multi-day ritualised celebration of freedom. At the same time, some of the partial events (especially those related to memorials and commemorations held at the sites of memory) are an opportunity for selected actors (from politicians of local, regional, or national importance through representatives of embassies of the celebrated countries to marginal local actors representing civic associations of little prominence) to instrumentalise these events. The symbolism of celebrated events, and the sites of memory and the political calendar associated with them (cf. Alexander 2006, p. 61), is thus a tool used by various actors to publicly (re)produce discourses and narratives that are significant from their perspective. Generally, it can be said that the main narratives (produced in various and often contradictory forms) are legitimised by references to the central myth carried by the festival – the myth of freedom. This myth (and the festival confirming it) is so strong and integrated into the Pilsen political sphere (and into the city's political calendar) that it bridges over even the

Fig. 2: *The Convoy of Liberty*

ideological paradigms identifiable at the level of the Pilsen administration – at this level, the relationship with the USA is strengthened by the fact that none of the political parties rejecting the transatlantic alliance (e.g. the communist or extreme-right political parties) has participated in the city's government in the post-November history. Of course, various political parties took turns as heads of the municipality, but they all had a positive view of the transatlantic alliance. This political constellation is also reflected in the form of the festival organised mainly by the city. Paradoxically enough, the festival can be perceived as one of the main platforms in which the Czech Republic's relationship with the United States is symbolically confirmed in a ritualised form. This is also one of the reasons why the top constitutional representatives of the Czech political scene and representatives of embassies (mostly ambassadors themselves) of the celebrated countries also participate in the central memorial events and commemorations.

Before we go into detail on the specific ways in which political actors instrumentalise the commemorations of the liberation and the end of the war in Pilsen, we can outline the structure of ceremonial events dedicated to memorial services and commemorations of the role of American (and Belgian) troops that serve as a platform for appropriately (re)interpreting the past and relating it to the legitimisation of current political visions and demands. Generally, we can say that the individual commemoration and celebration rituals are held ceremonially at the sites of memory, whose symbolism corresponds to the event itself – these are monuments to the Second World War, dozens of which are located in Pilsen and the surrounding area (as for the wider surroundings of the city and adjacent municipalities, we can speak of lower hundreds). These memory sites cover a wide range of events and actors that are commemorated, remembered and celebrated at the Liberation Festival – from war pilots through victims of bombings and uprisings to significant figures of the liberation and the U.S. military as a whole. Celebrations and commemorations take place primarily at such monuments that are conveniently located within the city's topography – in the squares and along the central thoroughfare called Klatovská Avenue,[55] connecting the southern and northern parts of the city.

---

55 This street can also be seen as a kind of geographical link connecting the central events of the Liberation Festival. This is, of course, due to its location and the role as the main highway in Pilsen. Additionally, this geographical connection has a symbolic dimension, because this is the route that a large part of the liberating troops took on their way to the city centre and the central square (this symbolism is even enhanced by the fact that, at the time of the liberation, the street was named Reinhard Heydrich Avenue after the former Protector of Bohemia and Moravia killed by Czechoslovak paratroopers). However, we perceive it as a geographical link because the whole dramaturgy of the celebrations (and the locations of the memory sites) de facto follows the street's line. The street's beginning is in the city part, where the largest city park in Pilsen is located, and where a provisional military camp was built during several years of the Liberation Festival organizing stationary demonstrations of war technology.

Every commemoration event usually consists of two parts – memorial service and speeches of political actors (local, regional, or national, depending on the nature of the commemorated event), representatives of the veterans, and civic initiatives. Ritual celebrations and commemorations then serve in a ritualised way as a tool for the (re)production of narratives associated with collective myths. Simultaneously, however, is it a platform that is significantly instrumentalised by the above-mentioned actors to confirm their symbolic authority (Apter 2006, p. 221) and for the purpose of (political) visions they promote.

As can be seen from the above, the Liberation Festival is a multi-day public event with a clear social and political significance. Dozens of partial events take place within the festival. From events that can be perceived as the main events, in which rituals of commemoration, memorial services, remembrance and symbolic connection of the past with the present are organised to events that can be perceived as side events, the content of which is primarily cultural, not political (cf. Goffman 1966; 2008). The variety of events is completed with the commercialisation of the festival using a wide range of consumer artefacts symbolically associated with the myth of freedom – from American flags through liberty beer and liberty burger to liberty whatever.

Given our professional anchoring in political science, the events that are key to our interpretation are such events within the festival that assume political significance. As has been stated several times, these events

---

A little lower, náměstí Míru (Peace Square) is connected to this street; there are three sites of memory, and commemoration events are held here. A few hundred meters below, the Chodské Square lies on the Klatovská Avenue, again with a memory site where events related to the Liberation Festival take place. A few streets below, Klatovská Avenue is crossed by the Americká Avenue with the central monument where the most massive commemoration and memorial events take place every year. Going further down the Klatovská Avenue, we pass the General Patton monument and we get to the Patton Memorial Pilsen where the street symbolically ends with the General Patton Bridge. Every year, a convoy of military vehicles (referred to as the Convoy of Liberty) goes down the Klatovská Avenue, symbolically copying part of the route taken by the Allied troops. With a bit of exaggeration (and if we borrow the line above), it is possible to perceive the Klatovská Avenue as "the most American street" in Europe.

are relevant to our research primarily for two reasons. On the one hand, they serve as a platform for the participating actors to raise and legitimise their political visions. On the other hand, the Liberation Festival can be seen as a central platform for ritual and ceremonial validation of the Czech Republic's foreign policy orientation and inclination towards the alliance with the USA. These factors can be considered as the reasons why top constitutional officials and authorities of the (not only) American representation in the Czech Republic take part in the festival every year.

The overall dramaturgy, symbolism and course of the celebrations are built around a specific narrative structure producing partial myths. This structure and the mythology derived from it is, of course, not only of limited and local (Pilsen) significance but can be largely generalised and applied to Czech society as a whole. Some of the partial myths that we will discuss in the following section are interpreted in the local context, but we believe they go beyond and apply to the whole society.

Narrative structure of the Liberation Festival

As mentioned before and as can be seen from the name of the festival, the narrative structure of the whole spectacle is closely linked to the (re)production and adoration of the myth of freedom. However, freedom is a concept that has its place in different political and ideological systems, and as a value, it is accepted (and adored) across the political spectrum, although its interpretations are, naturally, different (cf. Schwarzmantel 2008). Equally different are the partial myths that are (re)produced and strengthened during the festival and that are strongly linked to the central myth of freedom. This myth can be placed in a broader mythological structure, which we presented in the previous chapter. Freedom is one of the primary attributes of the Golden Age and can, of course, be ended by an occupation associated with the opposite – the myth of catastrophe and trauma. Subsequent liberation, the source of the new beginning of the Golden Age, is logically associated with the myth of revival. Occupation and liberation (and their bearers – metaphorical entities of liberators and occupiers) can be considered the foundations of the narrative structure around which the myth of freedom is built.

The following part of this chapter will interpret and explain in what forms and contexts the myth of freedom is (re)produced within the ritualised commemorations and celebrations organised as a public political spectacle. This part will also deal with how specifically the narrative structure is built by using metaphorical images of the past/present/(potentially) future liberators and occupiers. On the analysed example of the research field localised into one particular place associated with one particular festivity, we can illustrate how this public political event in the form of a ritualised commemoration, creation and reproduction of socially significant mythology has the potential to respond to current political topics (which are, naturally, completely detached from the original intention and connotation of the event). These conclusions about the instrumental use of history, to which this (and the following) chapter will be aimed, can, of course, be de-localised and transferred to a more general context.

Suppose we try to simplify everything that has been said about the festival in the most American city in Europe and generalise it as much as possible to the level at which partial narratives are (re)produced. In that case, it can be stated that the structure of the central myth of freedom consists of two major components: occupation (which ends freedom and establishes the Dark Age) and liberation (bringing freedom, ending darkness and establishing a new Golden Age). Within the specific political/cultural performances related to these cornerstones of the festival, specific narratives are (re)produced (narratives that can be understood as metaphors following the logic of "actor XY is an occupier/liberator"), and through them, the story of liberation or occupation is told.

Regarding the narrative structure and the dominant lines of liberation and occupation, it is important to note that the content of these categories is highly variable and dependent on the position of those who speak about these categories (and how the categories are perceived). The one who is perceived as a liberator by one actor can also be associated with the line of occupation by another (and vice versa). Various actors then use the symbolism of the commemoration events, their time and location (cf. Alexander 2006), in order to produce binary categories in a ritualised way and label the actors (metaphorically as well as explicitly) as liberators or occupiers (and, therefore, create and reinforce the image of the group as *the others*). In the next two subchapters, we will focus on the specific forms in which the festival's main lines – liberation and occupation – are narrated and how individual narratives are derived from these lines. During the festival, these narratives are reified, ritualised and celebrated by the actors, and they can be transferred from the local context to the context of the whole society.

Liberation

The liberation line is logically the most substantial element of the festival structure. This line's primary and central narrative is the metaphor "the USA is the liberator" (whether past, present or future).[56] This narrative permeates the whole festival and is reproduced by the participating actors without significant deviations (in the sense of the narrative's overall message). It is precisely this narrative, which is most strongly linked to the more general myth of freedom, that can be transferred from the context of the Pilsen festival to society as a whole, which is, after all, confirmed in the speeches of participating constitutional officials.

The notion of the "USA as the liberator" represents the core of the dominant discourse of the festival, and the United States along with the U.S. Army are, by the logic of the festival, the central actor whose adoration, celebration and commemoration are central to specific rituals related to the myth of freedom and its line of liberation. As mentioned above, the role of the U.S. as the liberator is not questioned by any of the relevant actors participating in the festival. The dominant part of the speeches made during the memorial and commemoration events greatly emphasises the role of the American army in the liberation and, generally, in the processes of spreading freedom and democracy.[57] However, the USA's role in spreading freedom and democracy is not understood and illustrated only in the local context (liberation of Pilsen in 1945) but is generalised and transferred to the level of the present and the global scale. In illustrating the American

---

56 The Belgian troops are always mentioned, however, in the "secondary role". In the other words, they are less visible than Americans, but still are included (contrary to the Polish soldiers – see below) among the liberators confirmed by the official narrative.
57 This can be illustrated by the example of one of the interviews with our informant, who told us that they see the adoration of the USA within the Liberation Festival as a duty of a local Pilsen politician.

role as an "omnipresent" actor embodying freedom and democracy, the connection to the NATO structures is often used to turn this myth from the past (1945) to the present.

This USA-NATO-freedom line is also often transformed during the festival into the line of argument that implies a certain responsibility/obligation for the liberated actor. This can be demonstrated, for instance, by the argument of one of the participating politicians,[58] who said that the American tanks brought freedom to Pilsen, but it took decades for their legacy to be fulfilled. Just as the Americans helped Czechoslovakia at the end of the war, the Czech Republic, as an integral part of NATO, will now help others to freedom. Therefore, according to the reproduced USA-liberator narrative, the American foreign policy brings freedom and democracy worldwide, and the Czech Republic should participate in this process through its involvement in NATO activities. Accordingly, the connection between the USA and the Czech Republic within the NATO structures is one of the platforms based on which the alliance of these two countries[59] is symbolically confirmed and validated during the festival. The manifestation of this alliance between the Czech Republic and the USA is one of the speeches' leitmotifs.[60]

It is evident that the "USA-liberator" narrative puts the United States in the position of the symbol of freedom. This symbol is represented within the festivities by various activities and artefacts – from displays of period technology and fashion through consumer and cultural production of the festival to the war veterans themselves, who get into the positions of theatre props in some of the festival's dramaturgy. Their function is mainly symbolic; they represent a reification of an American veteran (not just a

---

58 Jan Hamáček, at that time the Speaker of the Chamber of Deputies; delivered at a commemoration event at the Liberation Festival in 2015. The statement does not seek to capture the uniqueness of the argument, but rather illustrates the broader context in which the United States is mentioned during the commemoration rituals.
59 It can be illustrated with another quote from the speeches: "*Freedom must be fought for, and Czechs and Americans are allies in this fight*" (American veteran, 2018).
60 Noticeable, for example, in the figure: "*We will not forget what the USA did and sacrificed for Pilsen after the Second World War, and what they still do for us*" (Josef Bernard, then-governor of the Pilsen Region).

veteran of the liberation of Pilsen). This may support the timeless narrative that portrays the United States as the liberator. This timelessness of the American veteran was aptly played out during one of the festivals. One of the real veterans of the Pilsen liberation pointed out that due to advanced age, it is likely that the direct participants of the liberation will not be able to attend in the upcoming years. At the same time, he introduced his friend, an American veteran of the Korean War, who was also a member of the Second Infantry Division, which had liberated Pilsen and later fought in Korea. The Korean War veteran took over the symbolic baton. Once the direct participants are not available, they will be replaced by another category of American war veterans (having only a symbolic bond with Pilsen – an American veteran and a former member of the Second Infantry Division). However, since the figure of an American veteran (see Fig. 3) is key to the festival's dramaturgy and plays a vital role in the symbolic transmission and reification of the narrative portraying the USA as the liberator, the imaginary baton is being passed. It is a ritual aimed at preserving the "bearers of the liberation" – a specific tangible actor who would be placed in the form of a prop at a specific time to a specific site of memory.

With the following brief insert, we can illustrate the resistance and immutability of the central actors linked to the liberation line's interpretation. If the change was achieved and the liberators' repertoire was expanded to include the Holy Cross Brigade, the narrative structure of the liberation's interpretation would be complemented by the metaphor "Poles are liberators".

The American (and Belgian) troops were not the only actors involved in the liberation of Western Bohemia. During several years of the celebrations, the dramaturgy was influenced by another actor who also wished to earn their place among the category of liberators. This actor is the Polish Holy Cross Brigade.[61] Representatives of the historical association connected with

---

61 The Holy Cross Brigade was an anti-Nazi partisan unit that was linked to the Polish pre-war nationalist right and was strongly anti-German and anti-Soviet. After the USSR launched an offensive on Polish territory, the brigade set out across the Czech Protectorate with the aim of uniting with advancing Allied troops and not falling into Soviet captivity. At the end of the war, there were more than a thousand partisans in the territory of today's Pilsen Region, where, even before the arrival of American troops, they participated in the liberation

Fig. 3: *In 2021, when the presence of the US veterans was impossible due to the COVID-19 pandemic situation, their portraits were installed in the Pilsner parks instead of the presence*

this brigade repeatedly instrumentalised the symbolism of the commemoration events, their dates and venues to make a symbolic claim, which was contrary to the official narrative, dramaturgy and framing of the Liberation

---

of several villages and a women's concentration camp in Holýšov (about 20 km from Pilsen). These units did not reach Pilsen and were disarmed by American troops and moved to West Germany (despite the Soviets' requests for their extradition). Thanks to this decision, they avoided prospective internment in the Soviet gulags (see Friedl 2015).

Festival. We can interpret this actor's effort to enter the festival's dramaturgy as an effort to fulfil two goals. The first is the involvement in the commemoration events and the possibility of an official memorial ritual paying tribute to fallen comrades. This is followed by an effort supported by Poland's official representation in the Czech Republic, which aims to acquire space for creating a new site of memory dedicated to this brigade. In the general perspective, the two goals are connected by the effort to de-localise this episode from the end of the war and make it more widely known. The intentions are, therefore, to instrumentalise the ritualised commemorations of the liberation of Pilsen and to expand the foundations of their narrative structure by including the Polish side and granting a share to them. The (unofficial) involvement of these actors in the dramaturgy of the celebrations can thus be perceived as an attempt to exhume the memory (cf. Etkind 2013), and at the same time, as a potential disruption of the official dramaturgical and narrative line of the Pilsen festival. The Polish side's demands have not been accepted by the organizer, indicating the rigidity and immutability of the main narrative structure of the Pilsen Liberation Festival.

The resistance of the main festival's narrative can be illustrated, among other things, by an incident that occurred during one of the festival's commemoration events, when the police expelled several dozen period-uniformed members of the association from the site of memory. This intervention by power institutions de facto removing an undesirable element from the dramaturgy of the performed ritual was explained by the fact that the group was not an official participant of the festival. This particular intervention can be seen as a defence of the Liberation Festival's official narrative structure; the metaphor "Poles are liberators" has not become part of the festival's official discourse (both in the local context and the context of the whole society).

Occupation

The interpretation of occupation (the act that disrupted the existing freedom) is the second cornerstone of the Liberation Festival's structure. While the line of liberation is told through narratives about who (and why) is a "friend", the line of occupation stands in the Manichean position, producing mythologised images of who (and why) is the "enemy" (cf. Schmitt 1932). The primary narratives (re)produced within this line refer predominantly to such actors who, in the general perception, are portrayed (and socially perceived) as the historical (and in some contexts also contemporary) *others*.

Following the logic of the festival, the central metaphor present is "Germany is an occupier". The whole dramaturgy of the celebrations is based on the legacy of being liberated from the German occupation. Germany is thus the occupier, the architect of a national catastrophe, and an actor who ended the Golden Age, as which the interwar period is generally considered in the social perception. Therefore, the occupying actor established the Dark Age that was ended only by the act of liberation.

However, what is essential is a clear distinction about "which" Germany was really the occupier. Nazi Germany and its actions in 1939–1945 are framed as occupying. On the contrary, the current actions of Germany are framed as acts of alliance. Germany has thus succeeded in getting rid of the label of the occupier (also thanks to a strong social catharsis and work with its own past; cf., e.g. Evans 2015; Phillips 2001; Siegel & Harjes 2012). In the context of modern political development and the context of Czech foreign policy, the perception of Germany has been reframed in this way. The myth that Germany was an occupier, but today an ally, can again be generalised to the context of national politics. Although, from the perspective of the entire society, there are exceptions still portraying Germany as the potentially dangerous *other* (see the previous chapter). This view can be illustrated with a brief episode from one of the Liberation Festival commemoration events.

During a memorial act, a representative of the district organisation of the Czech Freedom Fighters' Union[62] framed the past and today's Germany as the ultimate evil, the enemy, and the embodiment of the absence of freedom.

---

62 It is an organisation that, based on its name, should bring together "fighters for freedom". However, the activities of this organisation are associated with politicisation, the membership of controversial church or political representatives, and power usurpation on their part. As a result, former members, including war veterans and the old-timer witnesses, are now leaving the organisation. The organisation was also significantly instrumentalizing the immigration crisis while its representatives joined the right-wing chauvinist politicians calling for defending Europe, building fences, deporting foreigners, and so on.

This organisation's representative built his speech on a simple narrative connecting the Second World War with the current political situation (or his perception of the situation). He began the speech with an appeal to the need to realise that Pilsen had not been liberated from German occupation only by American-Belgian troops, but the uprising of the people of Pilsen had also been a contribution, while many of these people had fallen, and only a few spoke of their legacy.

According to this presenting actor, they were the ones who enabled a smooth liberation. It is impossible to forget the legacy of the fallen people of Pilsen who faced the German threat. However, presumably, current Czech politics tramples their legacy with its contacts with Germany. According to this actor, the Czech construction of history is created based on political influence and does not sufficiently emphasise the German threat.[63] Furthermore, the Czech Republic devalues its sovereignty by negotiating with Bavaria as a federal state, thereby degrading itself to the level of a federal state, not a sovereign country. This brought him to criticise contemporary Germany's influence on the Czech Republic, leading the criticism in three lines. First, he criticised that the Czech Republic voluntarily accepted its position as a German colony, justifying this statement by saying that *"90 % of Czech exports flow to Germany"* (a very exaggerated estimate), thanks to which *"the Czech Republic is dependent on Germany"*. Second, he criticised the Sudeten Germans' alleged claims to have their property returned,[64] which can be interpreted as a warning against a possible strengthening of the colonial relationship. This is also evident in the third point of criticism – the Germans allegedly owning most of the Czech media, thanks to which they influence the Czech public opinion.[65]

---

63 The criticism of the rearranging of history is not unfamiliar to the Czech Freedom Fighters' Union. On their website, there is an entire section (called "That's not how it happened!") dedicated to the alleged rewriting of history, especially in relation to the war and Germany.

64 Again, a popular mantra of actors who portray Germany as the potentially dangerous *other*.

65 Given that the only major German media actor on the Czech media market at the time was the Bauer Media Group, which primarily owns leisure magazines for older ladies, this point of criticism was also unfounded.

Apart from the fact that this speech was based on disinformation and untruths, it was inconsistent with the overall mythological structure (whether local or society-wide). Several politically significant speakers opposed this speech, which can again illustrate the rigidity and unshakability of the festival's main narrative structure. The city authorities (i.e. the organizer of the festival) called the speech a disgrace. Among other things, the then-Mayor stated: "*We remember the positive end of the war, it is important to seek friends and partners and not to divide our society. This speech really does divide the society*". Then, the Deputy Mayor added: "*Some of the veterans and members of the foreign delegation understood this very well and were gracefully embarrassed. The question is whether to continue to maintain this cooperation with the Czech Freedom Fighters' Union*" (Beneš 2017). This can be interpreted so that the speech of the representative of the Czech Freedom Fighters' Union disrupted the dramaturgical and discursive structure of the dominant form of the myth of freedom. In this sense, although Germany has the label of a previous occupier, the war legacy has already been surpassed in this respect (reconciliation has occurred), and Germany is currently a partner.

The second narrative (re)produced during the festival can be easily generalised to the context of the whole society. This narrative can be articulated with the metaphor "Russia/USSR is an occupier".[66] While the United States is predominantly framed as a symbol of freedom, Russia acquires the opposite label and is often presented as a symbol of past, present and possibly future occupation. After the Russian invasion of Crimea, the mayor of Pilsen, Martin Baxa, stated in a speech given at the festival: "*The sovereign territory of Ukraine is once again curtailed and divided by the power of its neighbour, Putin's Russia. We can argue endlessly about the cause of this conflict, but the fact that cannot be circumvented is that sovereign Ukraine has lost, apparently for good, part of its territory, the Crimean*

---

[66] National Czech policy has long been somewhat inconsistent in the relation with Russia. While the government's attitude towards Russia has long been rather restrained, President Miloš Zeman can be, in many respects, considered a supporter of Russian interests (cf. Naxera & Krčál 2018). We have already discussed the standpoint of the Civic Democratic Party, of which the mayor of Pilsen is a member.

peninsula, and its other, eastern, part is essentially annexed". He then posted a photo from the event on his Facebook profile page, commenting that he had spoken that day at the Liberation Festival about Russia's danger to Europe. Already in this speech, Russia was depicted as someone who brings non-freedom. It is also worth mentioning that, in this speech, there was a warning against forgetting the events of 1968 that had brought the Soviet occupation to Czechoslovakia. He also pointed out that we still had to fight for freedom and democracy. This delineation in relation to Russia was also evident in the talk among the spectators who agreed that *"it was a pity that you* [Americans] *had not reached Prague"*.[67]

We have already mentioned part of the speech by Jan Hamáček, then-Speaker of the lower house of parliament, saying that the American tanks may have brought freedom to Pilsen, but it took several decades before freedom was actually achieved. This implicitly refers to the binarisation of the USA versus Russia/USSR position – while the "American tank" symbolises freedom, the "Russian/Soviet tank" symbolises occupation. Just as the American tank brought freedom in 1945, and still bringing it today (see above), the Russian/Soviet tank brought occupation in 1945 throughout Central and Eastern Europe, 1968 in Czechoslovakia, and now in Ukraine.

The liberation of Pilsen by means of the American tanks was only temporary – after 1948, meaning after the communist coup, the Soviet tank symbolically prevailed. In this interpretation, it is responsible for the continuation of the Dark Age. The Russian/Soviet tank as a symbol of a problem revealed itself in one particular incident of the last couple of years, which we refer to as the dispute over the "ideologically defective tank". We can start with the words of one of the organizers who confirmed in an interview that there were three different problems associated with the 2016 celebrations. They were unrelated, but they unfortunately coincided. According to our respondent, they created a "deadly cocktail" and helped to form the background of the ideologically defective tank story that aptly illustrates the metaphorical perception of the Soviet/Russian tank as a source of occupation.

---

67 This reaction of the audience is significant due to the fact that in the research of the festivities, the audience has the same actors' attributes as political representatives.

The first problem was the planned absence of the Convoy of liberty (see Fig. 2 above) mentioned above, representing a fundamental change in the celebrations' dramaturgy.[68] This was framed by part the public and the military fans negatively, and so a certain "convoy of defiance" was organised, standing outside the official celebrations' dramaturgy, and was met with minimal public interest.

The second and, in terms of symbolism and the sites of memory, a much more important problem was the dismantling of the Thank you, America! monument, whose central role in the commemoration rituals was described above. The monument was temporarily removed because the technical inspection revealed cracks in the granite structure, which was in danger of collapsing. It was only logical that, for safety reasons, the monument was dismantled before the festival started. In relation to the "Russia/USSR is an occupier" narrative, there were critical reactions on the part of some citizens accusing the city that the monument's removal at the time of the festival was an offering to Russia and an anti-American move. The symbolic value of the monument during the festival was also confirmed by one of the organizers, who told us in an interview that the city management had probably underestimated the situation and it would have been more appropriate if the monument's surrounding had been secured with a police tape, guarded by the police, and the monument removed only after the festival.

The last problem takes us back to the indicated metaphor related to the fact that the American tank is a symbol of freedom, while the Russian/Soviet one symbolises occupation. In this particular year, a Soviet tank was to participate in the festival. It was supposed to play a role in a re-enactment of a battle on the demarcation line.[69] From the perspective of the city officials

---

68 The main reason for replacing it with another programme was the fact that the convoy of the previous year, on the occasion of the "round" anniversary of liberation (2015), was completely unprecedented thanks to a massive involvement of modern American and Czech technology (that had been stationed for military exercise and was coincidentally returning through the Czech Republic at the time of the festival), and thanks to an increased presence of the vehicles from various military clubs – there were several hundred more vehicles than usual. So, the organizers wanted to prepare another event, not just a "flash in the pan" compared to the previous year's convoy.

69 The re-enactment of the battle was to be a spectator-attractive replacement for the cancelled Convoy of Liberty, and was to represent a certain mosaic depicting

and the organizers of this planned production, it was supposed to be a new and unseen show for the audience, and the potential presence of the tank was, of course, not ideologically motivated.

This brings us to the situation when all the above-mentioned components of the "deadly cocktail" (absence of the convoy, removal of the monument, and the ideologically defective tank) were discursively merged by part of the population and political actors into one line of interpretation framing these events as certain pro-Russian steps against the main spirit of the festival, which is meant to pay tribute to the Allied liberators. At this point, the clash of the two central narratives of the festival – the USA as a liberator versus Russia/USSR as an occupier – broke out in full. This clash and the complications associated with the celebrations resulted in a certain part (albeit marginal) of the Pilsen public referring to the festival's organizers as "communist bastards" and "monument destroyers" who were "fucking up the history".

However, what is more significant for political science than a few loud marginals on the Internet is the fact that the polarisation of the public was greatly intensified by the Pilsen organisation of the conservative party TOP09, which unleashed a strong wave of moral panic (cf. Cohen 2007; 2011) around the alleged rewriting of history by involving the Soviet (subsequently referred to as Russian) tank. The construction of the moral panic about the potential presence of a Soviet/Russian tank in the re-enactment of the battle can be illustrated with a statement published on the Facebook page of this party's Pilsen organisation: "*What do you think of the fact that this year the traditional exhibition of historical military technology, the Convoy of Liberty, will be missing during the celebrations of the Liberation Festival in Pilsen? Instead, the city management has newly included a battle of the Red Army in the celebrations' programme. [...] And why will the Red Army fight in Pilsen as part of the celebrations when we know from history that Pilsen was liberated by the American army?*" Then, the conservative party continued: "*We all remember how history was rewritten*

---

the events in the Czech lands before the end of the war. The staging production was to be conducted according to the following scenario (schematically outlined): The Soviet tank would be destroyed by a German tank, and then, an American tank would arrive and destroy the German tank.

under the previous regime. My peers and I learned at school that Pilsen was not liberated by the Americans but by the Red Army. For this reason, to me, it seems extremely inappropriate to have the Soviet soldiers participating in the May battle. We are quite sensitive about that here". A part of the Pilsen public criticised the conservative party for unleashing moral panic, also because the polarisation of the Pilsen citizens and the escalation of the situation resulted in the organizer of the re-enactment receiving threats of death.[70] The conservative party responded to the criticism and again continued with the line of deepening moral panic and primitive anti-Russianism: "[We refuse] *that we launched a campaign against the organizers of the celebrations of the end of the Second World War in Pilsen. Our concerns that efforts may be made to rewrite history are supported by the events of recent days and weeks [...]. That is why we were surprised by the active presence of Soviet technology at the festival*". The matter even resonated in the Chamber of Deputies.

The threats to the organizers were ultimately one of the reasons why the planned re-enactment of the battle was cancelled in the end. The tragicomical nature of the situation and how TOP09 instrumentalised the issue of the ideologically defective tank can be further emphasised by the fact that the exact same tank that was supposed to play a part in the re-enacted battle is present at the festival every year and serves as a stationary demonstration of the technology. In other words, the effort to set the tank in motion led to a political actor's bizarre text production, which helped to create a moral panic, polarise the people of Pilsen, and ultimately resulted in the cancellation of the planned production. All this happened behind the scenes of the "Russia/USSR is an occupier" narrative.

The last narrative associated with the occupation, which could be observed during the festival, and which is also applicable to the context of the society as a whole, can be simplified into the metaphor "immigration brings a threat of occupation". In the context of the so-called "migrant crisis", it was not unusual that the topic and the phenomenon of immigration became part of topics with which it had nothing in common. This relates to the fact that immigration is a phenomenon significantly securitised

---

70 Vulgar expressions were used towards him and his mother.

by political actors (cf. Bourbeau 2011; Žúborová & Borárosová 2016; Naxera & Krčál 2018, 2020a, 2020b, 2020c; Naxera 2019). This topic has also permeated the Pilsen Liberation Festival, for the first time in 2016.

The strongest line depicting immigration as a potential source of future occupation was led by the aforementioned representative of the Czech Freedom Fighters' Union, who stated that *"the wave of foreign culture rolling into Europe"* invalidates the legacy of people who fell during the Second World War while fighting for freedom. So, we won our freedom, and it is necessary to defend it from the invasion of *the others* who want to take it from us. Although this narrative is marginal within the Pilsen festival, it has strong societal contexts discussed in the previous chapter. Regarding immigration, the Czech political and social scene has been strongly polarised for several years; anti-immigration attitudes can be observed in many political parties, from democratic to the extreme right and left, and the instrumentalisation of immigration (a phenomenon that mostly eluded the Czech Republic) became central to the programmes of a number of political groups. Even several years later, the "immigration supporter" label is regularly used against opponents in the political struggle. However (unlike in the case of the SNU celebrations presented in the following chapter), at the Pilsen Liberation Festival, only the representative of an interest organisation (albeit politically strong), and not the participating politicians, spoke against immigration. On the contrary, a number of other participants (including the U.S. Ambassador or American veterans) pointed out the need for solidarity. It was one of the veterans who appealed that helping the war refugees of Syria to freedom is similar to the American troops helping the people of Pilsen gain their freedom. In the case of both different narratives associated with the so-called migrant crisis, an exemplary connection was made between the current situation and the celebrated event.

***

The narrative structure of the Liberation Festival consists of two main narratives that can be expressed through the metaphors "the USA is a liberator" and "Russia/USSR is an occupier". Although they are (re)produced in a narrow local context, they are firmly connected to the ideological framework of the whole society. The ties to the USA is mainly associated with the Czech membership in NATO. The opposition to Russia/USSR is related to the communist history and, especially, to the Soviet occupation of Czechoslovakia after 1968, as well as to current events in Ukraine. Both narratives also validate and confirm the foreign policy orientation of the post-Communist Czech Republic and the currently dominant framework for interpreting the communist past.

At the same time, it should be noted that in contemporary Czech politics, we find political currents that would like the Czech Republic to be more oriented towards Russia. These are not currents that would be politically marginal in any way – they are a whole range of actors, from President Miloš Zeman through the extreme left (the Communist Party of Bohemia and Moravia) to the extreme right (two parliamentary parties – Freedom and Direct Democracy and the Tricolour). We can also find the Russophile currents in other political parties. However, the Pilsen festival has long been organised by politicians who (at least declaratorily) express adoration for the alliance with the United States.[71]

The official narratives of the festivities are relatively permanent and are not subject to certain counter-narratives. As we have shown, some of these narratives, which are associated with defining oneself against *the others* discussed in the first chapter (especially against the Germans as historical and current enemies, and immigrants mainly from Islamic countries), are trying to disrupt the dominant line. They are unsuccessful in this regard. However, the (re)production of the official narratives and counter-narratives is supported by a similar argument, especially emphasizing fulfilling the legacy of the fallen soldiers who "did not die in vain". It fully shows the power of the political life of dead bodies (cf. Verdery 1999). This argument is amplified by the use of the symbolism of time (anniversary of the liberation) and place (site of memory related

---

71 In some cases, this gives rise to relatively specific situations. We can mention one speech by the former Governor of the Pilsen Region, Václav Šlajs, who before 1989 was an active member of the Communist Party and a politruk (ideological officer) in the Czechoslovak People's Army. Many years later, as a member of the Social Democracy, in his speech at the festival, he adored the alliance with the USA. After all, a similar trajectory associated with a specific interpretation turn is relatively typical for the post-communist countries.

to this liberation). The individual narratives then emphasise the need to defend freedom (against possible occupation), but these concepts are often interpreted from different perspectives. In the following section, we will see that the same principle is applied during the SNU anniversary celebrations.

Chapter 3 Slovak National Uprising as a "national treasure" and its annual celebrations in Banská Bystrica

The Slovak National Uprising (from now on referred to as the SNU) is one of the most pivotal events in modern Slovak history (cf. Mannová 2008). It was one of the largest partisan movements in Europe during the Second World War. Despite the military defeat, it gained a significant place in Slovak national mythology. The 29 of November, the day the uprising broke out in 1944, belongs among the most important national holidays in the Slovak Republic. The main celebrations are held every year on this day in Banská Bystrica, which was the centre of partisan operations; a number of memory sites related to the legacy of the uprising can still be found in the city and the surrounding area.

As in the previous chapter, we will introduce several interrelated themes connected with our research of the celebrations. After presenting the historical background of the celebrated event, we will look at least briefly at the history of the celebrations and commemorations of the uprising's anniversary. We will focus mainly on how the celebrations transformed along with the changes in the ideological framework. Unlike the Pilsen festival, the historical transformation of the SNU commemorations is often a topic among (not only) Slovak historians; as a result, we can rely on an extensive repertoire of sources. However, the main parts of the chapter will be based on our several years of field research – we will introduce both the organisational side of current celebrations and the related memory sites, and (especially) the narrative structure of the celebrations and political disputes over the use of the SNU's legacy for, among other things, negotiating the positions towards *the others*. Such disputes are a regular part of the celebrations (and have been since 1945, when the uprising and its legacy began to be significantly instrumentalised by political actors). For instance, we will show that, as in the case of the Pilsen festival, politicians use the SNU's legacy and celebrations to such things as warning against the Russian danger to contemporary Europe, but also to point out the need to cooperate with Russia. The chapter builds on some of our earlier works (Krčál & Naxera 2011; Naxera & Krčál 2016a, 2016b, 2016c, 2017a, 2017b, 2020a, 2020b), this text, however, is designed differently.

As mentioned above, the SNU forms one of the pillars of modern Slovak mythology. The annual celebrations and commemorations take place at a symbolic time and in a symbolic place (cf. Alexander 2006) – in the city that was the centre of the uprising and in the place where a museum and a monument stand today, commemorating this mythologically essential event. In terms of relevance to national mythology, it is a far stronger event than the liberation of Pilsen interpreted in the previous chapter. The liberation of Pilsen is, of course, also massively celebrated, and the basic narratives and myths produced within the celebrations can be generalised to the level of the whole society. However, this partial event did not penetrate the Czech national mythology with such a crucial significance as the SNU penetrated the Slovak mythology (cf. Syrný 2020).[72] So naturally, from the perspective of the instrumentalisation of history, the yearly celebrations involve the participating actors introducing topics that they legitimise with the SNU's legacy (and in the spirit of post-socialist political necromancy with the "dead bodies behind the uprising"). Even within the SNU celebrations, it is possible to identify the basic narrative structure, which produces myths and metaphors that can be de-localised and perceived as relevant to the whole society.

The reason why the SNU penetrated significantly into Slovak national mythology can be interpreted with another difference between the Pilsen case and Banská Bystrica. While the Pilsen narratives and the overall dramaturgy of the celebrations pay tribute to "those who brought us freedom on the barrels of tanks" (freedom that was guaranteed externally), the Banská Bystrica celebrations' narratives and dramaturgy pay tribute to "those

---

[72] This is reflected, among other things, in the participation of politicians. Although some constitutional officials speak at the Pilsen festival during memorial services, the whole celebration is the domain of local (or regional, at most) politicians who deliver most of the speeches. In Banská Bystrica, the centre of the festivity revolves around the highest constitutional officials and their speeches. Therefore, the Pilsen festival is a local or regional event, whereas the SNU anniversary celebrations have a national character.

who were one of us and fell for our freedom" (freedom guaranteed internally). The glorification of the SNU and its relevance for Slovak national memory can also be explained by the fact that by this act, Slovakia defined itself against the collaborating Slovak State and thus joined the side of the winners a year before the end of the war.[73]

Slovak National Uprising

> *The Slovak National Uprising does not need a defence. It is undoubtedly the most important historical event in Slovak history, which has been long defended by itself in the historical context.*
>
> —**Stanislav Mičev**, *director of the SNU Museum in Banská Bystrica (2020)*

The above quote, which was delivered by the director of the Slovak National Uprising Museum, and which, rather than to illustrate the view of one actor, represents a broader society-wide view, implies the significance of this event for Slovak national mythology. In the following lines, we will try to indicate at least briefly the basic contours of this event.

First of all, however, it is necessary to recall the context in which the uprising occurred. In the first chapter, we already indicated certain problems that accompanied the relations between Czechs and Slovaks within the joint state established in 1918. Since autumn 1938, meaning

---

[73] This act within the SNU (and de facto SNU as a whole) establishes a significant cleavage (cf. Lipset & Rokkan 1967) of modern Slovak politics. Namely, there is a dividing line related to the perception of the SNU. From the beginning of SNU commemorations, there has been an interpretation, which stands against the official (and socially accepted) narrative, and which frames this event as criminal, anti-national, pro-Czech, pro-Bolshevik, anti-Christian, or as an act of anti-state terrorism (Mannová 2019, p. 173). It is not surprising that such a perception of the SNU is dominant among the extremist political currents of the Slovak political scene, which we will look at in more detail on the example of the former governor of the Banská Bystrica region – the neo-Nazi Kotleba. After all, this whole dispute notably fits into the creation of binary categories (e.g. good vs. evil, Dark Age vs. Golden Age, truth vs. lies) that are typical for (not only) Slovak post-socialist national mythology (cf. Burzová 2014, pp. 72–73).

after the adoption of the Munich Agreement, Slovakia followed their own path, despite being de iure in a common state – in October 1938, they declared autonomy. With the "former Czech brothers" becoming *the others* and with the Italian-German fighting inspiration, their national mythology merged with Catholic conservatism (carried mainly by the dominant Hlinka's Slovak People's Party led by the later President Jozef Tiso from 1938 after the death of Hlinka) and, under the guarantee of Germany, the first independent Slovak Republic was proclaimed in March 1939 (Lupták 2009, p. 42). Although the state presented itself as an independent entity and its existence was recognised by a large number of the international community's members (e.g. Jakubec 2013), the geopolitical position of the state (Mičiniak 2003) and the considerable dependence on Germany cannot be ignored. It limited the room for manoeuvre of the Slovak political elite and relativised the independent statehood (Rosputinský 2016, p. 97). Slovakia's involvement in German military operations on the Eastern Front, the existence of the authoritarian regime, the enforcement of racial laws, including the expulsion of Jews and other groups of the population, and linking the economy with Germany, together with the Allies failing to recognise the state (acknowledging the Czechoslovak exile authorities in London as representatives of the entire Czechoslovak State) – all this brought nothing but the end of independent Slovak statehood (Lupták 2009, p. 43).

The year 1944 was, to a large extent, a year of Germany's defeats (not only) on the Eastern Front; at the same time, partisan movements were growing stronger in many occupied territories, the strongest ones in Yugoslavia and Slovakia. The coalition of states grouped around Germany also began to disintegrate – for example, at the end of August 1944, Romania terminated its alliance with Germany. Shortly after Romania denounced the alliance, Germany decided to seize Slovakia militarily since they no longer considered the Slovak government to be a reliable partner (cf. Stanislav 2020). The uprising, which broke out at the end of August 1944, also had a broader international context and a position within the negotiations between Moscow and the Czechoslovak exile in London, among other things, about the (ultimately unrealised) plan to join the uprising with the advancing Soviet troops.

Although the SNU began with considerable intensity and momentum, its strength gradually depleted, and by the end of October, the uprising was largely defeated, even though the guerilla fighting continued in the following months. The causes of the uprising being defeated include the technical and tactical superiority of German troops and the political disunity (internal and external) of the SNU preparation. The uprising claimed the lives of several thousand Slovak fighters and civilians, who became part of the ritualised remembrance, and the legacy of their death still has significant potential for consolidating national mythology (cf. Verdery 1999). As we will show in the following sections, it is the legacy of the fallen warriors that serves as a key argumentative and legitimizing tool for enforcing the political demands articulated during the annual celebrations.

After the uprising began, it was framed by the representatives of the collaborating regime as an event that broke out spontaneously, an event that was insignificant and, primarily, as an event that was the work of anti-Slovaks. The propaganda framework accommodating the needs of the Slovak State thus attributed the central role in the uprising to the anti-Slovak and anti-German elements, from Jews through Soviet paratroopers to domestic traitors. After the rebellion was defeated militarily, it was renamed to increase the propaganda impact (by creating a picture of the "great victory of Germans and Slovaks over anti-Slovak elements") – it was no longer referred to as a coup, and the term "uprising" began to be used instead (Mannová 2019, p. 173).

Although the uprising against the pro-German regime and German military power failed, it is crucial for the Slovak national mythology from a symbolic point of view. Resistance activities that culminated in the uprising, despite its military failure, miraculously managed to move Slovaks to the side of the victorious powers. Therefore, the Slovak Republic could be interpreted during the post-war division of collective guilt over the Second World War horrors as an excess of opportunists, fascists, the Catholic clergy, and other elements (cf. Lupták 2009, p. 43). After all, the fact that Slovaks were able to recognise evil and take the side of good in the most critical moment is regularly mentioned in the speeches delivered during the festivities.

History of celebrations and sites of collective memory

> *Great ideas, great revolutionary events in the lives of people and nations are also bridges from one epoch to another. The Slovak National Uprising was also a bridge from fascist enslavement, occupation and tyranny to national liberation, the restoration of our state, a bridge or at least the beginning of the journey from the epoch of capitalist exploitation, oppression and poverty of working people to the epoch of socialism, the epoch of the rule of the working people, the epoch of all-round development of our state. And there is a certain symbolism in that.*
>
> —**Gustáv Husák**, *President of the Czechoslovak Socialist Republic, speaking at a rally on the 28th SNU anniversary in Bratislava 1972 (quoted in Pažur, Chmelárová & Halaj 1979)*

The way the SNU is/was framed, presented, interpreted, celebrated and commemorated is, of course, subject to the ideological framework and to the specific way in which power institutions instrumentalise history. In this section, we will try to outline how the framing of this event and its celebration has transformed. Given that the SNU is an essential component of the collective memory of Slovaks,[74] the way how it is/was interpreted in official historiography and political discourse, or how it is/was socially perceived, is an important subject of Slovak (post)socialist political necromancy. So, regarding the SNU example, how specifically were the dead bodies evoked and instrumentalised?

In the years immediately after the war and before the establishment of the communist regime, a dispute between the democratically minded political current and the communist current began to emerge in the interpretation and framing of the SNU. The struggle for the interpretation of the SNU lasted throughout the whole period 1945–1948 (Michela 2020a, p. 316). The pro-democratic actors preferred the military significance of the uprising and the importance of the army's involvement. The military significance lies primarily in tying more than 50,000 German soldiers,

---

[74] This can be illustrated, for example, by the fact that the SNU is perceived by Slovaks as a predominantly positive event, and the central memory site dedicated to it – museum/monument in Banská Bystrica is one of the most strongly perceived symbols of Slovak statehood (Mannová 2008, p. 1).

who could not be deployed elsewhere at such a critical time but were positioned to suppress the uprising. The communist interpretation, on the other hand, creates a line emphasizing the role of the partisan units[75] and the people's nature of the uprising (Mannová 2019, p. 174). Generally, however, the SNU was framed (and commemorated during the first years of the celebrations) as an event that united the nation in the fight against Nazism (Mannová 2019, p. 176). As a nationwide connecting element, it was perceived at this time as a symbol of a new, post-war beginning, which was reflected in the sacral topography of its centre (Banská Bystrica)[76] by renaming the central square from Masaryk Square to the National Uprising Square (Michela 2020b, p. 28). Already in 1945, a memorial to the fallen heroes of the Soviet and Romanian armies was built in the middle of this square – on the site where several dozen soldiers who were killed during the liberation of the city and the surroundings were initially buried, and whose bodies were later transported to cemeteries in Banská Bystrica and Zvolen.

After the social and political changes of February 1948, the framing of the SNU changed as well (cf. Michela 2020a). There was a departure from the conception of the uprising as a national union in the fight against Nazism; official historiography and public commemorations began to build the image of the SNU as the beginning of the path to socialism. The role of the Red Army in the general liberation of Czechoslovakia began to be emphasised (Mannová 2019, p. 176). After 1948, the Communist Party gained a de facto monopoly on the instrumentalisation of the SNU's

---

75 This was also reflected in the way the SNU remembrance affected the physical sites of memory. Metaphorically, we can say that a non-party soldier (three times more of these fought in the uprising) gives way to an ideologically more appropriate communist partisan. There is a clear difference in their attributes demonstrated in the memory sites. While the soldier usually holds a rifle, the ideologically appropriate partisan is armed with a more ideologically appropriate Soviet machine gun (Mannová 2008, p. 4).
76 Banská Bystrica is also the location of the central monument and museum of the SNU, which was established in 1955. Since 1969, the museum has been housed in the grand building of the SNU memorial and focuses on museum activities, research, exhibitions, and cultural and educational activities (see Babušíková n.d.). Below, we will return to the museum and its building.

historical legacy, and the overall dramaturgy of ritualised commemorations was based on a basic narrative emphasizing the Soviet Union, on criticism of the bourgeoisie, and emphasis on the ideas of proletarian internationalism (Mannová 2019, p. 179). The SNU was seen mainly as the first step towards the country being liberated by the Red Army. This, of course, was reflected in period publications focusing on this event (e.g. Kropilák & Jablonický 1964; Pažur, Chmelárová & Halaj 1979). The monopoly on instrumentalisation and the exclusivity in creating the dramaturgy of the celebrations also manifested in the fact that ideologically inappropriate participants of the celebrations were excluded from the ritualised public commemorations. These commemorations and celebrations of the SNU were held without the members of the civil and non-communist resistance (Valko 2020, p. 37). Therefore, there was a significant reduction in the actors of the uprising since the commemorations were focused on only one segment of the resistance – the ideologically appropriate and adored communist resistance.

After 1948, the SNU and its legacy began to be instrumentalised and ideologically used[77] by the power institutions – a phenomenon that has persisted to this day in certain lines, which we will discuss below. The framing of the SNU as the beginning of the bright tomorrows of the socialist future is evident in a number of ways in which the SNU's legacy was (and in fact still is, albeit in a different ideological guise) handled – from ritualised commemorations, occupation of public space in the sacral topography of the country and cities (building physical sites of memory, renaming streets, etc.) to changes in the political calendar, and so forth (Mannová 2008, p. 4). The SNU is still recalled in the names of many important places in Slovakia – whether it is the central square in Banská Bystrica, nearby Zvolen, or in a number of other Slovak cities, including the capital Bratislava. In Bratislava, there is also the Slovak National Uprising Bridge built in 1972, one of the iconic landmarks of the city skyline.

---

77 This is aptly commented by Mannová, saying that the SNU's legacy changed from "fighting to building socialism" (2019, p. 183).

The ideological exploitation of the SNU potential is also evident in the effort to anchor it in pop culture with cinematography. In the socialist period, the topic of the SNU was highly addressed, and it represented the most frequent topic of Slovak film production. By 1989, more than 100 documentaries and 40 feature films had been made (Mannová 2019, p. 188) to support the official framing of the event. In addition to cinematography, the subject of the SNU was also used in less production-demanding formats, which, however, hardly concealed an open propaganda function – these were weekly film magazines. Their content and placing the events/actors in a juxtaposition with the SNU makes it possible to capture who was placed in the position of *the other* through the propaganda weekly magazines and who, on the contrary, fell into the category of *us*. For example, until 1948, the American soldiers were the ones positively portrayed. After 1948, this framing seemed ideologically inappropriate, and the adoration of the Soviet soldiers emerged instead, demonizing the American troops.[78] Therefore, it can be stated that the way in which the SNU was represented in cinematography and film weeklies reflected the transformation of the *us* and *the others* categories. The first category gradually changed to include the nation as a whole and later the communist-led people. The category of *the others* was filled with folk devils in the form of traitors, fascist Germans, West Germans, imperialists, capitalists, traitors of socialism (Mannová 2019, pp. 188–191). Thus, the basis for these *others* was ideological rather than ethnic.

The relevance of the SNU for Slovak collective memory, national mythology and its importance as a tool that enables supporting a wide range of political arguments is also emphasised in the sacral topography of Slovak municipalities, where more than half of political memory sites and monuments are dedicated to commemorating the uprising (Mannová 2008, p. 4). The central role is played by the aforementioned Memorial and Museum of the SNU (see Fig. 4) in Banská Bystrica, which is also the central venue of the annual celebrations.

---

78 Here, among other things, we find a parallel with how the celebrations and interpretation of the Pilsen liberation have changed.

Fig. 4: *The SNU Museum in Banská Bystrica*

The museum,[79] built in the 1950s and 1960s, is a free-standing building dominating the surrounding parks. The building consists of two concrete parts – these two parts and the divide between them stands for a symbolic breaking point and the tragic story of the war viewed from two sides. In the divide, there is a sculpture from 1969 titled "The Victims' Warning" (see Fig. 5) – the work was removed in the period of normalisation after the occupation of Czechoslovakia by Soviet troops in 1972 and returned to the museum in 2004. At present, the central memorial service and the laying of wreaths take place at this sculpture during the celebrations of the uprising anniversary.

---

79 The museum as an institution was founded in 1955 and joined the activities of the Institute of the Slovak National Uprising, which has existed since 1947. The museum moved to the mentioned building after its completion in 1969.

History of celebrations and sites of collective memory

Fig. 5: *The sculpture* The Victims' Warning *and the memorial site between the two parts of the SNU Museum building in Banská Bystrica (and Vladimír)*

While from 1948 until the end of the communist government in 1989, the SNU was interpreted as an event that was made possible mainly by the Communist Party and as an event that represents a milestone on the path to socialism (Mannová 2019, p. 186), after 1989, of course, the interpretation of the SNU and the manner of its political instrumentalisation changed significantly. After the fall of the communist regime, its monopoly on creating the historical legacy of the SNU died out. Public space, as well as political discourse, began to show the plurality in the framing of this event and its impact (which is also related to different perceptions of the Second World War Slovak State – it could be a Dark Age for some, but a Golden Age for others; cf. Naxera & Krčál 2016c). We can talk about two primary lines of demands that are being masked with the SNU's legacy – nationalist and civic. There is also an apparent delocalisation of the SNU's importance from the Slovak to the pan-European context based on the change in the course of Slovak foreign policy associated with the orientation towards the EU (Mannová 2019, p. 187). Thanks to the fall of Communism and the onset of the plurality of interpretations of the SNU's legacy, a wide space also opens up for the literature dealing with the SNU and its legacy, from fiction through educational popularizing texts to scholarly texts (see Fremal 2020). Therefore, it can be pointed out that the SNU and its legacy play an important role in contemporary Slovak politics, society and culture. As a result, we can say that the SNU's legacy and its instrumentalisation as a political relic is highly relevant even today. For example, the SNU is often used as a political argument in the context of events of the foreign and domestic scene (Mannová 2019, p. 194). In the following sections of this chapter, we will focus on how the SNU is instrumentalised by the current Slovak political representation and how specifically the dead bodies are evoked to support political demands (very often unrelated to the SNU).

Organisation and the course of celebrations

The premises of the SNU Museum in Banská Bystrica and the adjacent space are dedicated to the central celebrations of the SNU anniversary. It is also a primary site of memory related to the ritualised commemoration of the SNU. Sites of memory (and trauma sites related to them) serve as a tool for commemorating historical events associated with the constitutive milestones of national mythology. Therefore, it can be stated that the SNU Museum reproduces the meanings related to the event represented by the institution, and it gives them specific (e.g. victory, nation, homeland, freedom) and emotional content (cf. Oláh 2013). The emotionality and symbolism associated with this political festivity then allow these meanings to be instrumentalised by the participating actors.

Unlike the Pilsen festival, which lasts several days and takes place at a number of venues, the celebrations of Banská Bystrica are concentrated in a one-day event (with the cultural programme extended to more days) taking place at one venue. During the years 2010 and 2015–2019, when we attended the celebrations, the dramaturgy of the event was similar (with some exceptions) and followed the Goffman division of main and secondary events (Goffman 1956. The main event was a relatively short memorial service that was also broadcast live and held in the area adjacent to the museum building.[80] The memorial act consisted of the laying of wreaths by several dozen guests (national, regional and local politicians, ambassadors, representatives of the army and other security forces, representatives of social organisations, etc.). The wreaths were being laid in the museum's court by the sculpture "The Victims' Warning", and the laying was commented on and transmitted to the screen on the stage. At this stage, the speeches were delivered by the host (the Museum director Stanislav Mičev), constitutional officials (president, prime minister, Speaker of the Parliament, and usually also representatives of Romanian constitutional officials – Romanian troops participated, together with the Soviet troops, in the liberation of central Slovakia in 1945), and some other guests, accompanied by a cultural programme, mainly folklore. During the event, the entire area was delimited and, due to the participation of constitutional officials, there were security checks upon entry. After the end of the official part, which is usually watched by several hundred to a few thousand visitors, there was a cultural programme going on until the evening.

The accompanying programme also takes place in another of the adjacent park areas, where the period military equipment (German, Soviet, and Czechoslovak) is permanently located. During the celebrations, there is a presentation of the activities of the Slovak army whose members participate in the celebrations in large numbers; it is possible to buy refreshments, military literature, models of the military equipment, and so forth. The legacy of the fight for freedom is thus commodified not only on a symbolic level (within the political speeches, when freedom is understood as "goods" exchangeable for political arguments) but also on a completely explicit level (the sale of snacks, souvenirs, etc.). The celebrations also include military flyovers, paratroopers performing paradrops, or a massive military parade that took place in 2019 on the occasion of the 75th anniversary.

It is interesting that during the years of celebrations, it was possible to observe some attempts to disrupt the dramaturgy and the dominant

---

80 An exception was the year 2019, when, due to the 75th anniversary of the uprising, the event was attended by a larger number of guests and was moved to the adjacent park located below the slope under the museum building – the museum thus created a dominant feature located on the hill behind the venue of the memorial programme.

Fig. 6: *Supporter of the "Charter 2015" initiative with a banner "We don't want NATO bases, weapons and troops in Slovakia" during the SNU anniversary celebrations in Banská Bystrica*

interpretation of the whole event. These attempts were in some cases related to the figure of former Slovak Prime Minister Robert Fico – some of his speeches were accompanied by loud protests of his opponents. Even more interesting, however, were the attempts to disrupt the tone of the whole event – among others, the celebrations are regularly attended by (a small number of) members of the long-marginal Communist Party of Slovakia (cf. Kopeček 2007) dressed in the political party's T-shirts, often with banners condemning Slovak foreign policy and NATO participation. Although they question the current direction of Slovak politics, they do not question the importance of the SNU, in which the communist partisans actively participated and are therefore perceived as part of the uprising. During some of the celebrations' years, the supporters of the "Charter 2015" (see Fig. 6) also appeared – it was an association led by former officials of the Communist Party of Slovakia, including former agents of the Communist secret police. The movement presented itself as anti-fascist, anti-war, and pro-peace, criticizing NATO and Slovakia's involvement in the organisation, along with their adoration of Russian policy, including the Soviet past.

The second similar case is related to the neo-Nazi party People's Party Our Slovakia (cf. Voda, Kluknavská & Spáč 2021; Naxera et al. 2020; Maškarinec & Bláha 2016; Kluknavská & Smolík 2016; etc.), whose leader Marián Kotleba comes from Banská Bystrica and for several years he held the position of a directly elected head of regional government. Since the party is one of the actors adoring the Slovak State and questioning the legacy of the SNU, it also refuses to participate in the celebrations. During some of the years' ceremonies, for example, Kotleba hung black banners from the window of his office in the upper part of the SNU Square, along with signs questioning Slovakia's engagement in NATO. In the following section, we will return to the role of Kotleba and his party in the discourses associated with the celebrations in even more detail.

Narrative structure of the SNU anniversary celebrations

Like the ritualised adoration of the myth of freedom in Europe's most American city, the annual celebrations of this national treasure (as Fico titled the SNU in 2015) contain a basic narrative structure that we will follow in the section below. Like the narrative structure of the Pilsen Liberation Festival, the one of the SNU's commemoration is primarily related to the myth of freedom. However, the myth is framed differently here. While Pilsen commemorates freedom imported to Pilsen and guaranteed externally, political festivities in Banská Bystrica focus on celebrating the freedom that was fought for from within, with a united effort of the nation, that is, freedom guaranteed internally. What is similar is the principal form of the central myth of freedom, which has two main lines – the line of liberation and the line of occupation, both shaped by their individual narratives and metaphors. As in the previous chapter, we will try to interpret several years of SNU's annual celebrations in terms of how the participating actors narrate and frame who is/was/can be an occupier and which actors acquire the attributes of liberators. Concerning these categories created by constitutional officials, we will also point out the conflicts of interpretation that proved to be even more profound than the disputes during the Pilsen celebrations. As we will show, different interpretations of the perception of threats or allies were being created mainly by the former Prime Minister Robert Fico.

Liberation

The line of liberation is quite logically related primarily to the uprising's participants and to the fact that the SNU was an event that tried to liberate Slovakia from Nazism (in the end, at least symbolically by allowing Slovakia to side with the Second World War winners). Therefore, it is clear who is the liberator in this narrative – the Slovaks. Although this main line of the liberation narrative has remained resistant to manipulation and modification by power institutions and their changing ideological needs, it is important to point out that the content (and scope) of who was included in the category of liberators changed significantly over time – from the Slovak nation as a whole through the army and the partisans (later "cut" to the ideologically desirable communist partisans) to the return of the nationally conceived liberation. The question of whether the SNU and the liberation linked to it were perceived as a manifestation of external or internal liberation was also subject to instrumental modification. As indicated in the previous section, the communist regime framed the SNU and the liberation narrative as freedom that came "from within" but was also a preview of a "greater freedom" that came "from the outside", followed by the path to the bright tomorrows of socialism. After the fall of Communism, this narrative of liberation prevailed and is ritually confirmed every year at the SNU celebrations – liberation came (or is supposed to have come) from within the united Slovak society. The fact that Slovakia was subsequently liberated by the Red Army is not being questioned during the celebrations. At the same time, it is a topic that has been mentioned rather marginally in recent years of the SNU anniversary celebrations. The actor who regularly praised the role of the Red Army was the former Prime Minister Robert Fico, who did not hesitate to use the legacy of the liberation of Slovakia as an argument for closer cooperation with Russia. However, we will get to this subject below.

Furthermore, it is worth pointing out certain counter-narratives to this dominant and socially accepted liberation narrative. The most important is the interpretation of the SNU that follows the line of its framing as a negative event, as something that was led by anti-state elements and attacked the legitimate Slovak state. This interpretation is predominantly held by right-wing extremists and is well captured with the approach of neo-Nazi

Marian Kotleba, who was a governor of the Banská Bystrica region and ignored the SNU celebrations from his position, or symbolically disagreed with them (e.g. by hanging the black banner from the governor's building during the festivities). In the dominant discourse, the SNU was an attempt to regenerate the nation with the goal (ultimately unsuccessful) of ending the Dark Age and restoring the Golden Age. In the interpretation of (not only) Kotleba, on the other hand, the period of the Slovak State was the Golden Age – the SNU was therefore an attempt to end this age and throw the country into a period of darkness.[81]

The legacy of the SNU and its victims framed as heroes who placed the ultimate sacrifice on the altar of freedom, together with the fact that the SNU is a central component of contemporary Slovak national mythology, allows the participating political actors to use the celebrations to support their political demands. This can be illustrated by some statements of political actors. Specifically, these are the statements by which the participating actors characterised the SNU in such an image that they subsequently used to support their own political goals.

It will be most appropriate to start with illustrating how the former Prime Minister Robert Fico framed the SNU during one year of the celebrations: *"The Slovak National Uprising is a national treasure that a member of every nation and country would be proud of. This gem allows us to speak the truth"*. Thus, the historical legacy incorporated into Slovak national mythology gives the right to interpret current events and make moral judgments. Subsequently, Fico used this SNU framing to produce the narrative of occupation (see below). Similarly, then-President Andrej Kiska also characterised the SNU and its relevance, saying that the uprising is proof that *"Slovakia can recognise evil"*. Kiska subsequently referred to the fact that, despite the SNU failing to succeed militarily, it won the battle for the character of Slovakia, giving the current state moral energy and strength. A final example of the political[82]

---

81 We can mention another example of counter-narrative – the still influential Catholic church. It representants idealize Slovak state collaborating with Hitler and tries to reach the canonization of its president Tiso. The church officials do not participate in the celebrations.
82 The SNU is not framed in this manner only by the participating political actors, but also by actors who are unpolitical. For example, the commentator of the

framing of the SNU relevance and legacy, and how political actors prepare their ground for categorizing *the others* and those who, according to them, represent the main sort in the line of occupation and its individual narratives, can be the characterisation of the SNU and evocation of its victims by the part of Peter Pellegrini (then-Speaker of Parliament elected in the Banská Bystrica region). He spoke of the legacy of ancestors making the right decisions during the war cannot be neglected; the SNU was the result of their decisions. Such an ancestral legacy and sacrifice cannot be disappointed, which is why today's Slovakia must make the right decisions in addressing current security challenges. Pellegrini also said that the Slovaks, as one of a few nations, fought on all the Second World War fronts and, thanks to the SNU, contributed to Hitler's defeat.

Generally, the characterisation of one of two central lines of the SNU ritualised commemorations – the line of liberation – can be concluded by the fact that the dominant narrative currently (re)produced in the annual celebrations in Banská Bystrica presents the liberation to be brought from within, with significant involvement of the Slovak resistance fighters. And it is the fallen resistance fighters, soldiers and civilians, whose dead bodies are evoked, called forth and used by political actors to support the (political) arguments they make, which (as we will show below) often unrelated to the commemorated event. Metaphorically speaking, the army of dead resistance fighters, soldiers and ordinary Slovaks who fell when fighting in the SNU is sent by the political necromancers to fight *the others* who are framed as a potential source of occupation. Thus, political actors significantly instrumentalise the politics of dead bodies (Verdery 1999) to construct the Manichean relationship between the two central lines of the mythological structure linked to SNU – line of liberation and line of occupation. In the following section, we will look in more detail into which actors/phenomena are instrumentally associated with the occupation standing in contradiction to glorified liberation.

---

celebrations mentioned that *"the Slovak National Uprising is a connecting link from the beginnings of our statehood in the time of Great Moravia to today's statehood. This linking arch is a struggle of Slovaks for their national and cultural identity"*.

Occupation

Given the Czech and Slovak society's geographical and cultural proximity and the similar orientation of foreign policy, it is not surprising that the line of occupation and individual narratives and metaphors (re)produced during the SNU celebrations largely overlap with similar narratives of the Pilsen festival. As part of the SNU's commemoration, the metaphors "Russia/USSR is an occupier" (extended with the metaphor "Russia/USSR is the liberator"; see below) and "immigration is a source of potential occupation" are also produced. Thanks to the context of the celebrations and the specific political constellation[83] that de facto determined the discursive form of several years of celebrations, it is possible to observe another metaphor falling into the line of occupation – "extremism is a source of occupation" associated with the metaphor "extremism tramples the legacy of the SNU". The last metaphor that can be captured within this line is the metaphor "Is the EU (not) a friend?" which in some lines strongly follows the metaphor associated with immigration. After introducing the basic metaphors of the narratives of occupation, we will now take a closer look at how specifically these metaphors are created by the participating actors.

However, before we look at the above-mentioned metaphors in more detail, it is important, as in the case of the Pilsen festival, to begin with the relationship with (Nazi) Germany. As with the Pilsen celebrations (excluding politically irrelevant marginals from the Czech Freedom Fighters' Union), Nazi Germany as the main occupier, whose defeat is the subject of both celebrations, is defined as an enemy on an ideological (rather than ethnic) basis. In the case of the SNU, therefore, the uprising was both an uprising against Nazi Germany but also (and this is a more important element for Slovak national mythology) against a government that collaborated with evil. Germany and the Germans are constructed as *the others* within the SNU mythology primarily on an ideological basis; the current negative framing is exclusively related to the Second World War.[84]

---

83 Neo-Nazi as the head of the region in which the second largest anti-Nazi uprising of the Second World War broke out.
84 Although, as shown above, in the case of the instrumentalisation of the SNU's legacy by the communist regime, the Germans and Germany were framed as *the others* on both an ideological and ethnic basis.

From the relationship with Nazi Germany, we can move on to one of the metaphors above – "extremism tramples the legacy of the SNU". This metaphor resonates most strongly in relation to the already mentioned neo-Nazi Marián Kotleba,[85] who was the governor of the Banská Bystrica region in 2013–2017. Within this metaphor, the figure of Kotleba is used by other political actors as a certain point of reference, whose actions are both beyond the limits of politically acceptable normality and also tarnishing of the glorified legacy of the SNU.

The metaphor describing extremism as tarnishing the legacy of the SNU is an integral part of annual festivities, but in 2017 it took the form of some of an anti-Kotleba discourse. This was primarily due to the fact that a few months after the SNU celebrations, new regional elections were held in Slovakia, in which Kotleba (unsuccessfully) tried to defend his governor mandate. The host of the event, Stanislav Mičev,[86] emphasised the importance of the SNU Museum as an institution *"holding the flag of anti-fascism"*, and he framed the SNU with an emphasis on commonality and unity of action against the fascists[87] – both historically and based on

---

85 Marián Kotleba is the leader of the right-wing extremist/neo-Nazi party Kotleba – People's Party Our Slovakia (cf. Maškarinec & Bláha 2016). On the one hand, this party follows and refers to the tradition of the war-time Slovak state, to which Kotleba proudly commits. On the other hand, Kotleba presents himself with actions that have a clear link to neo-Nazism (for which he is currently being prosecuted) – for example, there was Kotleba's gift of €1488, where the numbers 14 and 88 are obvious neo-Nazi symbols (cf. Mareš 2006). Kotleba's party, with regard to its extremist/neo-Nazi character, thematised the issues that are in fact expected from such an entity – from Slovakia's relationship with the EU (with a request to leave the EU) through efforts for historical revisionism to the topic of immigration, whose potential threat Kotleba significantly instrumentalised (cf. Voda, Kluknavská & Spáč 2021).
86 Director of the SNU Museum and at the time of the festivities in 2017 also running against Kotleba as his rival candidate for the office of governor.
87 Individual speakers repeatedly used the terms fascist/Nazi and fascism/Nazism as synonyms. In our interpretation, we try to keep their vocabulary, and therefore we do not make an analytical distinction between the two. Although from the perspective of political science, these are different ideological and value systems, in the narrative structure of the analysed event and the metaphors contained in it, they have the same meaning – evil that brought (and can bring again) occupation.

the need for unity against neo-Nazi Kotleba: "*There are many of us who express our support for anti-fascism and freedom. We are united, and it will remain that way*". So, there was a call for united action against Kotleba and his party. Anti-fascism and the need to bring the Banská Bystrica region out of the political isolation caused by Kotleba were the leitmotifs of Mičev's campaign.

The then-President Andrej Kiska continued in a similar vein, explicitly speaking against the collaborating regime: "*The Slovak State faithfully served the Nazi and fascist ideology [...]. The heroes of the uprising understood that it was impossible to retreat from evil and survive with one's head bowed, hoping that the criminal Third Reich would pass away on its own or be defeated by someone else [...]. The participants of the uprising won respect for Slovaks [...]. Thanks to the uprising, Slovakia can build on civic and democratic foundations*". He then used the (by him or generally) glorified legacy of the uprising to criticise the neo-Nazi Kotleba and his followers: "*It is not enough to commemorate and give speeches when there is a spawn of fascism roaming around. When the fascist won, it was a shock for Banská Bystrica. It was even more shocking when he got to the Parliament. We are trying to deal with this and respond to the fascists. What hatred lies behind their smiles and green T-shirts. Their only contribution to the public debate is the spread of hatred. He can intimidate and bully; he can't manage public affairs*". He then moved from criticizing Kotleba and his neo-Nazi supporters to instrumentalizing the SNU and its legacy to mobilise the electorate: "*We will stand up to evil and expel the fascists from the governorship in Banská Bystrica. Kotleba considers the beginning of the SNU to be the blackest day in Slovak history, his only contribution being the spread of hatred. Region after region, we must not hand over our beautiful country to the fascists. We do not have to fight with arms in hand, we do not have to be heroes, it is enough if we are real citizens, and we participate in democratic elections, and we choose a non-fascist candidate. There are more of us, and we can defeat them, and at the same time, we can draw on the courage of those who resisted evil under incomparably more unfavourable conditions*". Thus, the mobilisation rhetoric included the instrumental use of the SNU's legacy, where going to the polls and voting against the fascists is a certain analogy of the anti-fascist fight. If the ancestors were able to stand up to the fascists with a weapon in hand and a willingness to risk their own lives, then the least that Slovaks can do to honour their memory is to come to the elections and vote for democratic actors.

The metaphor related to extremism and transformed into a specific anti-Kotleba discourse was also reproduce by another participating political actor, the then-Speaker of the Parliament, Andrej Danko. He also used the symbolism of the SNU's legacy and drew a parallel between the Nazis and Kotleba's neo-Nazis, calling on voters to *"evict the Nazis from the governorship by coming to the polls. Let's not allow lunatics to control the state power"*. For the sake of completeness, let us add that Andrej Danko is the chairman of the strongly right-wing and nationalist Slovak National Party. The last actor, at whose speech we will look in relation to the anti-extremist metaphor, is the then-Prime Minister Robert Fico. He began by recalling *"what Slovakia looked like at the time when the Slovak State existed as a servant of Hitler. People lived here peacefully, but Nazis and the Hlinka Guardists were walking around, and it was also Slovaks who participated in this. And nearby* [the celebrations' venue], *there is a building in which they again use the "On guard!"*[88], *and we somehow feel that it's all right"*. Like previous speakers, he drew a parallel between past and present (neo) Nazis and pointed out that expelling current neo-Nazis was not as risky and dangerous as the situation in which the SNU participants acted. He ended the speech by returning to the explicit criticism of the neo-Nazis: *"Freedom of speech does not mean using the Nazi salute and shouting "On guard!", and so on. I call on law enforcement authorities to take action"*.

The metaphor "extremism tramples the legacy of the SNU" is firmly integrated into the narrative structure of SNU's annual commemorations. The participating political actors regularly define themselves against extremism (most often in the form of neo-Nazism). In 2017, the dead bodies of partisans and SNU participants were significantly politically evoked to be used as a shield for the existing political need to unite the electorate in order to remove the neo-Nazi political actor from the region's government. Kotleba's neo-Nazi party eventually lost the regional elections (not only in

---

88 "On guard!" was a salute used by the Slovak Nazis in the period of the Slovak State.

Banská Bystrica region, where Kotleba lost in the direct election of the head of the regional government), which Andrej Kiska commented: "*I am very glad that the extremists got beaten on Saturday. We defeated hundreds of their candidates in all regions with our strongest weapon – free voting in democratic elections*".

The second metaphor that can be observed in several years of the SNU commemorations, and which was most strongly present (similarly to the case of the Pilsen celebrations) in 2015 and 2016,[89] is the metaphor "immigration is a source of potential occupation". This metaphor can, of course, be very easily de-localised (whether from the Banská Bystrica of Pilsen area) and related to the general Slovak (and Czech, in the case of Pilsen) context. The SNU's legacy was used to frame the phenomenon of immigration in two main lines, which also reflected the current social division regarding this matter.

On the one hand, some arguments used the legacy of the SNU to call for treating potential immigrants in solidarity. Andrej Kiska's statement can be the example: "*I don't think that much is required of us, our country. We know we are not the destination. There are no big demands on us; and our contribution to our Europe, the European Union, is to show solidarity with people whose lives are really in danger in their country and who need help*". During his speech at the celebrations, he emphasised that such an attitude is the fulfilment of the SNU's legacy. In a similar spirit, the then-Speaker of the lower house of the Romanian Parliament[90] continued, saying that "*what is happening in European countries today could, without a swift and vigorous action, become the biggest humanitarian catastrophe after the Second World War*". In his speech, he also rejected the fake news that accompanied the so-called migration wave – that they are merely economic migrants (cf. Miller 2016).

For the intent of our book, however, what is more important is the second line of argument, which was produced in relation to immigration

---

89 Thanks to the culmination of the medially and politically produced moral panic regarding the "migrant crisis".
90 As we have said, Romanian constitutional officials usually take part in the celebrations because Romanian troops liberated central Slovakia together with the Red Army.

and which de facto constructed the content of the metaphor "immigration is a source of potential occupation". The topic of immigration is a frequent subject of securitisation (cf. Bourbeau 2011; Krotký 2019), and the context of Slovak politics is, of course, no exception in this respect (see Androvičová 2015; Naxera & Krčál 2020a; Žúborová & Borárosová 2017). This negative framing of migration was logically reflected in the fact that some participating political actors instrumentalised the SNU's legacy to support such arguments that would have negative attitudes towards immigration, even securitizing it in some positions. Probably the most prominent critic of immigration and a supporter of the "closed borders" policy was the then-Prime Minister Robert Fico. He also significantly instrumentalised the legacy of the SNU and connected it with the issue of immigration, which he framed as a security threat. Fico spoke about the fact that fascism was a threat that Slovakia dealt with thanks to the SNU, and now a new threat had emerged, the threat of immigration. It is, therefore, necessary that Slovakia does not disappoint the legacy of the SNU and can face this threat as well. Fico then pointed out that, on the one hand, the position of refugees was deplorable, but on the other hand, it was necessary to protect *us* (Slovaks/Europeans), not *the others*. It is, therefore, not possible to risk European/Slovak security for the protection of refugees. "*Let's not pretend we don't see people's fears. They are afraid not only in Slovakia but in the whole of Europe. Let us not pretend not to see the causes of this phenomenon, and let us not pretend to be able to solve this problem by welcoming everyone with open arms, whether they are economic profiteers or people who really need protection for their lives, health and families*". The semantic emphasis on fear and the fact that people are afraid can be interpreted in the intentions of politics of fear, where political actors use the symbolism of time and place of a specific event to produce fear, which very easily transforms into political profit (Altheide 2002, p. 6). Subsequently, Fico spoke against domestic opponents of his view, calling them "*pseudo-humanists welcoming refugees*". Then, he spoke against the European Union as a whole: "*Europe is facing an uncontrollable flood of refugees from different parts of the world. European migration policy has completely failed.* [... Uncontrolled] *migration can destroy Slovakia and Europe. Let's be honest, because we are not able to integrate our own Roma fellow citizens, of whom we have hundreds of thousands. How can we integrate people who are, moreover, somewhere else entirely, both in terms of way of life and religion?"* At the end of his appearance, he very cleverly incorporated the SNU's legacy into his speech, saying that *"traditions, values and democracy must be protected, and if we do not protect them sufficiently from immigrants, the fascist and Nazis, who will tackle this problem differently, will win the election. Those against whom the Slovak National Uprising was led will win"*.

The metaphor portraying migration as a source of danger (and potentially domination of the non-native, and thus occupation) is reproduced on several levels[91] by the then-Prime Minister Fico. First of all, it is an economic threat (economic migrants, whose very presence damages the state economy), then a threat to the culture and values (cf. Czajka 2014; Mukhin 2015) due to cultural differences and the impossibility to integrate the (alleged) newcomers. Furthermore, there is a potential threat to physical security and, last but not least, the influx of immigrants may tarnish the SNU's legacy by reinforcing extremist tendencies in society that would subsequently result in voting for the neo-Nazi party. On the other hand, it should be noted that Robert Fico, the long-term leader of the Smer Party, which presents itself as a social democracy, but is a typically populist and anti-immigration party (Naxera et al. 2020), was one of the vocal critics of immigration (albeit in 2018–2017, the criticism of immigration was Slovakia's mainstream, from which perhaps only President Kiska deviated). At the same time, Fico proposed actions that were on the edge of liberal democracy (or even beyond) – an example is his plan to monitor all Muslims in Slovakia by secret services (cf. Žúborová & Borárosová 2017). In other words, the combination of the SNU's legacy with the anti-immigration rhetoric has served two parties, both anti-immigration, in the fight for voters.

How the SNU's commemoration and legacy were used in 2015 and 2016 to securitise immigration can be concluded with the speech delivered by the then-Speaker of the Slovak Parliament Peter Pellegrini, saying that today's Europe is facing three security threats. The first of these is the already mentioned immigration (however, he did not address this issue any further). The

---

91 Again, we should remind that this is a metaphor that can be very easily related to the context of the whole society (both Slovak and Czech).

second threat that Europe has to deal with is the war situation in Ukraine. The third source of potential threat is Russia and its foreign policy. From this, we can move smoothly to the last pair of metaphors that are (re)produced within the individual occupation narratives during the festivities, and that can be related to the general social context. These are metaphors associated with the role of Russia/USSR and the European Union. It can be stated that these two metaphors have been an integral part of the dramaturgy of the SNU celebrations since the beginning of the commemorations and have always been significantly dependent on the ideological context of the time period in which they appear. As we showed in the section focusing on the history of the celebration and the transformation of its basic narratives, the SNU commemoration always has, in a ritualised form, confirmed/rejected the relationship of Slovak society to Russia/USSR/Europe/European Union.

We will also analyse these metaphors together, given that their framing has been considerably interconnected by participating actors in recent years. Russia's positive framing is often accompanied by the negative framing of the EU (and vice versa). This binary relationship is symptomatic of how Russia or the EU are perceived by the society. Metaphors related to Russia and the EU were also significantly connected in some years (2015 and 2016) with the migration-related metaphor interpreted above. Robert Fico spoke very extensively about the Slovakia-Russia-EU relationship. He also elaborated the already mentioned characterisation of the SNU being a national treasure allowing Slovaks to speak the truth with the argument that one of these historical truths is that, in Munich,[92] Czechoslovakia was sold by the West. The legacy of the SNU was used in this way to define oneself against the West, which subsequently turned to criticism of the EU (especially in relations to the migrant crisis, see above). According to Fico, EU policy clearly represents a potential security threat to Slovakia (and thus fits into the metaphor of a potential source of occupation). This threat stems mainly from the European Union's approach to migration and Russia. The EU/Slovakia's relationship with Russia was also evident at the 2016 celebrations, when Fico symbolically followed the arguments outlined above, saying that he was concerned that some Slovak

---

92 See the "Munich betrayal" illustrated in Chapter 1.

and European politicians were looking for an enemy on whom to blame all their problems. He stressed that he rejected the antipathies brought into the Russia-Slovakia relations and the fact that Russia is accused of being the cause of all problems. According to Fico, the one who does this is the EU. It was clear from the context of the speech that the European Union is the one who frames Russia in this way. Fico also warned of a possible escalation of the conflict between Europe and Russia (let us add that it was shortly after the beginning of the conflict in eastern Ukraine). Then he inclined towards the metaphor depicting the USSR/Russia as liberators, pointing out that the Soviet Union had the lion's share in the defeat of Nazism. It is, therefore, not possible to make contemporary Russia an enemy. Thus, in Fico's interpretation, the historical event from more than 70 years ago is directly reflected in his support of the current political demand, that is, closer cooperation between Slovakia and Russia.

Regarding the metaphors "Russia/USSR is an occupier/liberator" and "EU is a friend/enemy", we find two primary lines of interpretation (which are selectively illustrated here, however, as mentioned above, they can be generalised to the whole context of Slovak and also Czech political scene and social dividing lines). The first is the designation of Russia as a security risk (including a possible occupation with reference to what is happening in Crimea and eastern Ukraine). The second is the perception of the EU as a potential source of danger (due to immigration, the impending conflict with Russia, etc.). Both of these lines of interpretation are, of course, complemented by the arguments of other speakers, who portrayed these actors positively. Robert Fico was de facto the only constitutional actor across the year of celebrations who called for closer cooperation with Russia and warned against European Union policies. On the contrary, most other speakers at individual celebrations drew attention (at least implicitly) to the threat of Russian aggression for Europe and the need for Slovakia's strong involvement in European (as well as transatlantic) structures. At the end of this section, we can illustrate how the SNU's legacy is linked to Europeanism. For example, then-President Andrej Kiska pointed out during one year of celebrations that *"thanks to the uprising, we can stand here as proud citizens of the republic and free Europeans"*. In fact, this is the same approach used by Robert Fico, supporting a possible re-orientation of current Slovak foreign policy with the statement about the Soviet part in the results of the war.

***

The narrative structure of the last years of the SNU anniversary celebrations in Banská Bystrica consists (as in the case of the Pilsen festival) of two central lines – the line of occupation and the line of liberation. However, individual narratives (re)produced by the present officials are somewhat more diverse than in Pilsen. Even in Banská Bystrica, the partial narratives and metaphors correspond to the currently valid ideological framework. Nevertheless, while in Pilsen, the counter-narratives were created mainly by marginal actors (representatives of the Czech Freedom Fighters' Union or the Polish Historical Association), during the SNU celebrations, the overall message was disrupted mainly by former Prime Minister Fico, who, unlike other speakers actively emphasised the security context of migration, the need for emancipation from the EU policy, and greater ties with Russia. To support these demands, he used the SNU's legacy. After all, similarly to most other speakers, who used the SNU's legacy to support Slovakia's Western orientation, cooperation within the EU, vigilance against Russia, and solidarity with migrants.

Finally, it is necessary to mention another counter-narrative, although unspoken during the celebrations and manifested by the absence of the then-leader of the Banská Bystrica region, the neo-Nazi Marián Kotleba. While Robert Fico did not question the primary mythological structure that the SNU was an attempt to defeat the Dark Age (although he used this interpretation to support political demands different from those of other actors), Kotleba fundamentally rejects this vision – the SNU's success would not bring an end to the Dark Age, it would instead lead to it.

Conclusion

Remembering, commemorating, celebrating, forgetting, ignoring – these are all concepts associated with the instrumentalisation of history and memory. Political work with memory must reflect its two primary components. These are soft memory, which is built on a textual and discursive basis, and hard memory, which is a "tangible memory" anchored in the sites of memory, that is, in monuments, museums, statues, or in the sacral topography of cities and landscapes (cf. Etkind 2004; 2013). Both components are considerably interconnected and cannot work without each other. Alexander Etkind (2004, p. 40) mentions in this context that *"the hardware of historical memory – for example, monuments – stay mute and, practically speaking, invisible unless they are discussed, questioned, interpreted; in other words, unless they interact with software, which is the current intellectual and political discourse"*. In the case studies discussed in this book, one focusing on the local celebrations of external liberation and the other on central celebrations of internal liberation (or the effort),[93] we sought to capture exactly how the software and hardware of the commemoration rituals based on a symbolic adoration of the myth of freedom are interconnected. Our effort was to present the fundamental narrative structure of these political festivities. The structure (see Tab. 1) is based on two primary components – occupation and liberation, which then produce narratives including metaphorical depictions of who was/is/can be a liberator/occupier. Basically, all the images constructed in this manner can be de-localised from the Pilsen/Banská Bystrica terrain that we examined and applied to the level of the society as a whole. The same clashes

---

[93] Apart from the fact that in one case the liberation came from the outside and in the other it is supposed to have come from within the society, we find the difference in who was the source of the previous non-freedom. While in the case of the Pilsen celebrations, it is a struggle against the external enemy (the Nazi Germany), the SNU went against both the Nazi Germany and the regime of the Slovak State. The fact that the uprising was led not only against *the others*, but also against the regime that emerged from *us* as a category has a number of implications – for example, the existence of a not entirely marginal political current that sees the uprising as a betrayal.

that could be identified in the speeches delivered during the celebrations simultaneously take place (to a greater or lesser extent) at the level of the entire political community (although some of the views are borne only by marginal political currents).

The narrative structures of the Pilsen Liberation Festival and the Banská Bystrica commemorations often overlap. They do so even though the position of the two analysed political festivities is different. The festival in Pilsen represents local celebrations of the myth of freedom (guaranteed externally) related to the final stage of the war. High constitutional officials attend the festival, but the dominant political actors are politicians of local/regional importance. However, the scope and symbolic meaning of this event exceed its local character, as a large part of the narratives and the metaphors contained in them can be related to the context of the whole society. Apart from the ritualised affirmation of the relationship between the Czech Republic and the USA, it is mainly the depiction of the USSR/Russia as a potential source of future occupation. The narrative regarding the perception of immigration as another source of potential occupation[94] can also be de-localised and applied to society's context. The overall message of the festival, its symbolism and narratives can very well be anchored in a myth that is symptomatic of (not only) Czech national mythology (see the first chapter) – the myth of the Dark Age (Williams 1997, p. 135). However, the age of national suffering was not ended by a celebrated event, and therefore the Golden Age could not be reached (cf. Smith 1997). From this perspective, another Dark Age was established under the supervision of Soviet tanks after a short post-war intermission; it was ultimately ended with a national revival in the form of events of the end of 1989. Just as the German tanks were bringing non-freedom in 1938–1939, so were the Soviet tanks in 1948–1989.

It is the narrative "Russia/USSR as an occupier" as a contradiction to the narrative "the USA as a liberator" that can be illustrated by the metaphorical expression portraying the American tank bringing freedom and the Russian/Soviet tank being the omen of occupation. The relationship to contemporary Russia and its political actions forms one of the cleavages

---

94 In relation to the escalating migrant crisis in 2015–2016.

Tab. 1: Summary of the narratives

	Pilsen		
LIBERATION	The USA as a liberator	The main narrative associated with liberation; the US is seen as a source of past, present and future freedom; applicable to the context of the whole society (despite the existence of a number of anti-American currents in Czech politics)	
	Poles as liberators	A narrative disrupting the overal dramaturgy of the commemorations; it failed to assert itself	
OCCUPATION	Germany as an occupier	In the context of the whole society, from a historical perspective, Germany (primarly on the ideological basis, it means the Nazis) represents one of *the others*, i.e. enemies; currently a narrative valid rather in the marginal parts of the political spectrum (on the contrary, the dominant political representation, including the participants in the celebrations, consider contemporary Germany as an ally), however, there is a discussion at the level of the whole society	
	Russia/USSR as an occupier	The main narrative associated with occupation during the celebrations; a topic significantly polarizing the Czech society and the political scene; applicable to the context of the whole society	
	Immigration brings the threat of occupation	A narrative instrumentalised during the so-called migrant crisis; a topic significantly polarizing the Czech society and the political scene; it constructs an image of the dangerous *others* applicable to the context of the whole society	

(continued)

Tab. 1: Continued

	Banská Bystrica	
LIBERATION	Slovaks as liberators	The main narrative associated with liberation; significantly ideologically modified in the historical context; currently, there is a "counter-narrative of betrayal"; applicable to the context of the whole society
	Russia/USSR as a liberator	The secondary narrative of liberation; promoted by selected political actors (but not questioned by others)
OCCUPATION	Russia/USSR as an occupier	A narrative instrumentalised by selected political actors; a topic polarizing the Slovak society and the political scene; applicable to the context of the whole society
	Immigration as a source of potential occupation	A narrative instrumentalised during the so-called migrant crisis; a topic significantly polarizing the Slovak society and the political scene; it constructs an image of the dangerous *others*; it constructs a discourse of a potential threat to the SNU's legacy; applicable to the context of the whole society
	Extremism trampling the legacy of the SNU	The main narrative of the occupation; extremism must be fought = fulfilment of the SNU's legacy; applicable to the context of the whole society
	The EU as a friend/enemy?	A narrative instrumentalised, among others, during the so-called migrant crisis; linked to the potential threat to Slovakia from immigrants; applicable to the context of the whole society (there are currents questioning Slovakia's involvement in the EU and its current activities)

visible in today's Czech society (and the Czech political scene). Both the society and the political scene are divided based on their attitude to Russia.[95] We illustrated some of these tendencies in the first chapter. During the festival, the references to past friends and enemies (liberators and occupiers) are thus being related to the present.

At the level of the society, it is clear that some political currents (such as the parties representing the far right and far left) that are pro-Russian (and often largely nostalgic for the era of the USSR) are both anti-German, anti-American, and anti-immigrant. However, these circles have not yet been represented at the Pilsen festival – so, during the celebrations, there are no conflicts of opinion that we can observe at the parliamentary level.

The annual ritualised commemorations of the SNU's legacy are by their nature a far more significant event for Slovak national mythology than the Liberation Festival is for Czech national mythology. After all, the Liberation Festival remains largely a local affair, although some narratives (as we have shown) can be de-localised. The SNU celebrations represent an event that has a nationwide character, takes place with the participation of high constitutional representatives, and is broadcast on Slovak public television.[96]

The SNU represents one of the most important events in modern Slovak history and is instrumentalised and framed (in all dominant interpretations) as an event that terminated (or tried to terminate) the Dark Age and marked the beginning of the Golden Age of the Slovak nation (cf. Smith 1997). On the other hand, there is a counter-narrative that understands the period of the Slovak State as the Golden Age and the SNU as an attempt to disrupt it

---

95 It is important to mention here that we are finishing the book at a time when the Czech intelligence services came with the information that members of the Russian GRU unit are behind the explosion of the ammunition depot in the Czech Republic in 2014. Thus, there is a significant polarisation of the relations between the Czech Republic and Russia. At the same time, the event activated a number of political actors (President Miloš Zeman, the parliamentary far right and far left) who began to question the work of the Czech intelligence services and to frame Russia as a partner, not an enemy.

96 Which often alters its standard program during the commemorations and broadcasts programmes related to the SNU – from documentaries and feature films, through news and debates, to travelogues such as "Cycling in the footsteps of the uprising".

and establish the Dark Age. This counter-narrative was present during the years of celebrations that we examined mainly by the symbolic absence of the leader of the Banská Bystrica regional government, the neo-Nazi Marián Kotleba, who, above all, carries these attitudes in contemporary Slovak politics. It is Kotleba and his party who are, at the level of the society, the actors disrupting the narrative dominant during the celebrations – the idea of Slovaks as liberators.

In addition to agreeing on the narrative depicting Slovaks as liberators, there is a consensus among the politicians participating in the last years of the celebrations rejecting political extremism (mainly right-wing extremism), which tramples the SNU's legacy and aims to bring a new Dark Age, that is, the age of non-freedom. However, in the case of other narratives, there were significant disputes among the celebrations' participants (exceeding the ones during the Pilsen festival), which copy, to a large extent, the division going on at the national level. If we simplify the conflicts, we can describe them, with some exaggeration, as "Robert Fico versus the rest". In his speeches, former Prime Minister Robert Fico made political demands (e.g. associated with immigration, Russia, or the EU) that were opposite to those of other participants. The SNU celebrations thus reveal a lot about Slovak national politics.

Returning to the metaphor of Alexander Etkind (2004; 2013) that memory work has its software and hardware side, we can declare that although the hardware of the events we examine differs significantly, their software component is very similar. Both events (or the symbolism, narratives, and metaphors contained in them) penetrate into the national mythology of both political communities (albeit to a different extent). If we simplify the software scheme of both examined events, we can say that political necromancers evoke the dead bodies of the veterans (Czech, American, Slovak, Soviet, and more) in order to send them to fight alleged political enemies representing a source of potential occupation. The fact that both events use the politics of dead bodies (cf. Verdery 1999) to (re) produce narratives and metaphors that are also applicable to the political or society's context allows their significance to go far beyond their local geographical anchoring. By penetrating into national mythology, some of these presented narratives/metaphors are naturalised by the society/political representation and thus perceived as natural (Overing 1997, p. 5). In this manner, they become a component of collective memories, and their instrumentalisation is one of the tools used for the legitimisation of power institutions and their past/present/future political demands (Allison 2015, p. 906).

Thanks to the political and social relevance of the celebrated events, the narratives they produce and the metaphors that these narratives contain, transcending into the cultural and commercial spheres, it can be stated that both the SNU celebrations and the Pilsen Liberation Festival leave an imprint in all components of collective memory – public, official, and vernacular (cf. Breuer & Delius 2017, p. 459). In the public component of collective memory, the examined events resonate mainly in the sense that they represent a dominantly accepted interpretation of "what happened" and determine its significance for contemporary politics and society. In the official component of collective memory, it is possible to identify the resonance of the examined events in that they are associated both with specific sites of memory and with political festivities dedicated to their commemoration. And lastly, the vernacular memory resonates in the fact that both the SNU celebrations and the Pilsen Liberation Festival, or the myths they carry, imprint themselves (albeit to a different extent) into national mythology, especially in relation to the binary opposition between the myth of the Dark Age and the myth of the Golden Age (cf. Smith 1997).

Epilogue

Pilsen – spring 2021

Petr: At the time of finishing the manuscript of this book, I took a walk with the pram and passed by one of the sites of memory in Pilsen. The same place I walked by in the winter, and where I noticed the dog's grave. During that time, I found out that it was a Labrador Retriever named Vincent, and his human family often remembered him because candles were almost always burning at his grave and flowers were changed regularly. During one of the walks, instead of the new (but already mundane) silhouette of Vincent's site of memory, there was another view for me – a view of the city's technical crew clearing away the remains of the dog and removing this public place for private remembrance of a dog family member. The site of memory was thus purified from undesirable elements of memory.

***

This brings us to the central argument of this book (and academic discussion related to the instrumentalisation of history in general) – who is officially commemorated, remembered, celebrated, forgotten, ignored, and damned is always a political act expressing the will of power institutions. And it does not matter if it is a dead dog, a dead partisan, a dead soldier, or an otherwise instrumentalised dead body. (Post)socialist political necromancers decide when and which bodies will be evoked and which, on the contrary, will be cast into oblivion.

List of figures

Fig. 1: The patch of the Second Infantry Division that participated in liberating Pilsen (left) and the Pilsen ice hockey club logo introduced in 2009 (right) 65
Fig. 2: The Convoy of Liberty 66
Fig. 3: In 2021, when the presence of the U.S. veterans was impossible due to the COVID-19 pandemic situation, their portraits were installed in the Pilsner parks instead of the presence 74
Fig. 4: The SNU Museum in Banská Bystrica 96
Fig. 5: The sculpture The Victims' Warning and the memorial site between the two parts of the SNU Museum building in Banská Bystrica (and Vladimír) 97
Fig. 6: Supporter of the "Charter 2015" initiative with a banner "We don't want NATO bases, weapons and troops in Slovakia" during the SNU anniversary celebrations in Banská Bystrica 100

Bibliography

Abăseacă, R. 2018, 'Collective memory and social movements in times of crisis: The case of Romania', *Nationalities Papers*, vol. 46, no. 4, pp. 671–684.

Alexander, J. 2006, 'Cultural Pragmatics: Social Performance Between Ritual and Strategy', in J Alexander, B Giesen & L Mast (eds), *Social Performance: Symbolic Action, Cultural Pragmatics, and Ritual*. Cambridge: Cambridge University Press, pp. 29–90.

Allison, S. 2015, 'Residual history: Memory and activism in modern Poland', *Nationalities Papers*, vol. 43, no. 6, pp. 906–926.

Altheide, D. 2002, *Creating Fear: News and Construction of Crisis*. New York: Aldine de Gruyter.

Althusser, L. 2014, *On the Reproduction of Capitalism: Ideology and Ideological State Apparatuses*. London: Verso.

Anderson, B. 2016, *Imagined Communities. Reflections on the Origin and Spread of Nationalism*. London: Verso.

Androvičová, J. 2015, 'Sekuritizácia migrantov na Slovensku – analýza diskurzu', *Sociológia*, vol. 47, no. 4, pp. 319–339.

Anušauskas, A. 2012, 'Politics and History in Lithuania', in Z Krasnodebski, S Garsztecki & R Rüdiger (eds), *Politics, History and Collective Memory in East Central Europe*. Hamburg: Reinhold Krämer Verlag, pp. 99–108.

Apter, D. 2006, 'Politic as Theatre: an Alternative View of the Rationalities of Power', in J. Alexander, B. Giesen & L. Mast (eds), *Social Performance: Symbolic Action, Cultural Pragmatics, and Ritual*. Cambridge: Cambridge University Press, pp. 218–256.

Assmann, A. 1999, *Erinnerungsräume. Formen und Wandlungen des kulturellen Gedächtnisses*. Munich: Verlag C.H.Beck.

Assmann, A. 2006, *Der lange Schatten der Vergangenheit. Erinnerungskultur und Geschichtspolitik*. Munich: Verlag C.H.Beck.

Assmann, A. 2007, *Geschichte im Gedächtnis. Von der individuellen Erfahrung zur öffentlichen Inszenierung*. Munich: Verlag C.H.Beck.

Assmann, J. 2001, *Kultura a paměť. Písmo, vzpomínka a politická identita v rozvinutých kulturách starověku*. Praha: Prostor.

Auerbach, Y. 2004, 'The Role of Forgiveness in Reconciliation', in Y Bar-Siman-Tov (ed), *From Conflict Resolution to Reconciliation*. Oxford: Oxford University Press, pp. 149–175.

Babušíková, T. Undated, História múzea, viewed April 9, 2021, < http://www.muzeumsnp.sk/muzeum-snp/historia-muzea/>.

Bar-Siman-Tov, Y. (ed) 2004, *From Conflict Resolution to Reconciliation*. Oxford: Oxford University Press.

Barthes, R. 1972, *Mythologies*. New York: Macmillan Publishers.

Bartošek, K. & Pichlík, K. 1953, *Američané v západních Čechách v roce 1945*. Praha: Mladá fronta.

Benazzo, S. 2017, 'Not All the Past Needs to Be Used: Features of Fidesz's Politics of Memory', *Journal of Nationalism, Memory & Language Politics*, vol. 11, no. 2, pp. 198–221.

Beneš, R. 2017, Vedení města Plzně kritizovalo ostudný projev předsedy svazu bojovníků za svobodu při pietním aktu v rámci Slavností svobody, viewed March 15, 2021, <https://www.zaktv.cz/zpravy/5076-vedeni-mesta-plzne-zkritizovalo-ostudny-projev-predsedy-svazu-bojovniku-za-svobodu-pri-pietnim-aktu-v-ramci-slavnosti-svobody.html >.

Beránek, O. & Ostřanský, B. (eds) 2016, *Stíny minaretů. Islám a muslimové jako předmět českých veřejných polemik*. Praha: Academia.

Berlin, I. 1969, *Four Essays on Liberty*. Oxford: Oxford University Press.

Bernstein, S. 2015, 'Remembering war, remaining Soviet: Digital commemoration of World War II in Putin's Russia', *Memory Studies*, vol. 9, no. 4, pp. 422–436.

Biesecker, B. 2002, 'Remembering World War II: The rhetoric and politics of national commemoration at the turn of the 21st century', *Quarterly Journal of Speech*, vol. 88, no. 4, pp. 393–409.

Bookman, M.Z. 1994, 'War and peace: The divergent breakups of Yugoslavia and Czechoslovakia', *Journal of Peace Research*, vol. 31, no. 2, pp. 175–187.

Bourbeau, P. 2011, *The securitization of migration. A study of movement and order*. London: Routledge.

Breuer, L. & Delius, A. 2017, '1989 in European Vernacular Memory', *East European Politics and Societies and Cultures*, vol. 31, no. 3, pp. 456–478.

Bureš, J. 2019, 'Prezident viník? Edvard Beneš a Únor 1948 v kontextu učebnic dějepisu', *Střed/Centre*, vol. 11, no. 1, pp. 32–79.

Burzová, P. 2014, *Okouzleni pohledem na dav. Principy uzavření a meze postsocialistické slovenské identifikace*. Praha: Sociologické nakladatelství.

Burzová, P., Dvořáková, I., Hejnal, O., Růžička, M. & Toušek, L. 2013, 'Paměť a prostor: Reprezentační strategie společenstva vzpomínání v postindustriálním městě', *Sociální studia*, vol. 10, no. 4, pp. 107–126.

Busbridge, R., Moffit, B. & Thorburn, J. 2020, 'Cultural Marxism: far-right conspiracy theory in Australia's culture wars', *Social Identities*, vol. 26, no. 6, pp. 722–738.

Čechurová, J. 2018, 'Svátkový kalendář ve světle legislativní činnosti, in D Hájková, P Horák, V Kessler & M Michela (eds), *Sláva republice! Oficiální svátky a oslava v meziválečném Československu*. Praha: Academia, pp. 45–72.

Chlup, R. 2020, 'Competing myths of Czech identity', *New Perspectives*, vol. 28, no. 2, pp. 179–204.

Cingerová, N. & Dulebová, I. 2020, 'Rock Beats the Wall? On Commemorative Practices in Post-Soviet Russia', *Journal of Nationalism, Memory & Language Politics*, vol. 14, no. 1, pp. 71–91.

Cohen, C 1989, 'Free speech and political extremism: How nasty are we free to be?', *Law and Philosophy*, vol. 7, no. 3, pp. 263–279.

Cohen, S. 2007, *Visions of Social Control. Crime, Punishment and Classification*. Cambridge: Polity Press.

Cohen, S. 2011, *Folk devils and Moral Panics. The Creation of the Mods and Rockers*. Oxon: Routledge.

CVVM, 2016, *Občané o odsunu a Benešových dekretech. Tisková zpráva Centra pro výzkum veřejného mínění*. Praha: CVVM.

Czajka, A. 2014, 'Migration in the Age of Nation State: Migrants, Refugees, and the National Order of Things', *Alternatives*, vol. 39, no. 3, pp. 151–163.

D'Orsi, L. 2015, 'Trauma and the Politics pf Memory of the Uruguayan Dictatorship', *Latin American Perspectives*, vol. 42, no. 3, pp. 162–179.

Dvořáková, V. & Kunc, J. 1994, *O přechodech k demokracii*. Praha: Sociologické nakladatelství.

Encyklopedie Plzeň, 2019a, Americká, viewed February 24, 2021, < https://encyklopedie.plzen.eu/home-mup/?acc=profil_ulice&load=210>.

Encyklopedie Plzeň, 2019b, Wilsonův most, viewed February 24, 2021, < https://encyklopedie.plzen.eu/home-mup/?acc=profil_domu&load=80>.

Eriksen, T.H. 2006, *Antropologie multikulturních společností. Rozumět identitě*. Praha: Triton.

Eriksen, T.H. 2010, *Ethnicity and Nationalism. Anthropological Perspectives*. London and New York: Pluto Press.

Esterling, S., John-Hopkins, M. & Harding, Ch. 2020, 'Reflections of International Justice as a Commemorative Process', in C Gilbert, K McLoughlin & N Munro (eds), *On Commemoration. Global Reflections upon Remembering War*. Berlin: Peter Lang, , pp. 51–58.

Etkind, A. 2004, 'Hard and Soft in Cultural Memory: Political Mourning in Russia and Germany', *Grey Room*, no. 16, pp. 36–59.

Etkind, A. 2013, *Warped Mourning: Stories of the Undead in the Land of the Unburied*. Stanford: Stanford University Press.

Evans, R.J. 2015, *The Third Reich in History and Memory*. Oxford: Oxford University Press.

Forchtner, B. 2016, *Lessons from the Past?* London: Palgrave Macmillan.

Fremal, K. 2020, 'Odborná a náučno-populárna literatura o odboji a SNP v rokoch 2017–2019', in M Syrný (ed), *Slovenské národné povstanie – medzi minulosťou a odkazom pre dnešok*. Banská Bystrica: Múzeum Slovenského národného povstania v spolupráci s Katedrou histórie Filozofickej fakulty UMB v Banskej Bystrici, pp. 61–70.

Friedl, J. 2015, *Vojáci – psanci. Polská Svatokřížská brigade Národních ozbrojených sil na českém území v roce 1945*. Praha: Vojenský historický ústav.

Frýbertová, T. 2014, 'Nedáme si diktovat, koho máme milovat. O sletovém průvodu v roce 1948', *Theatralia*, vol. 6, no. 1, pp. 52–89.

Fukuyama, F. 2018, *Identity: The Demand for Dignity and the Politics of Resentment*. New York: Farrar, Straus and Giroux.

Garsztecki, S. 2012, 'Memories of the Holocaust and the Jewish heritage in Belarus and Poland', in Z Krasnodebski, S Garsztecki & R Rüdiger (eds), *Politics, History and Collective Memory in East Central Europe*. Hamburg: Reinhold Krämer Verlag, pp. 197–219.

Gilbert, C. 2020, 'Introduction: Words Fail Us', in C Gilbert, K McLoughlin & N Munro (eds), *On Commemoration. Global Reflections upon Remembering War*. Berlin: Peter Lang, pp. 13–21.

Gilbert, C., McLoughlin, K. & Munro, N. (eds) 2020, *On Commemoration. Global Reflections upon Remembering War*. Berlin: Peter Lang.

Goffman, E. 1956, *The Presentation of Self in Everyday Life*. New York: Doubleday.

Goffman, E. 1966, *Behavior in Public Places: Notes on the Social Organization of Gatherings*. New York: Free Press.

Goffman, E. 2008, *Interaction Ritual. Essays in Face-to-Face Behavior*. New Jersey: Transaction Publishers.

Grynevych, V. 2012, 'The Myth of War and the War of Myths', in Z Krasnodebski, S Garsztecki & R Rüdiger (eds), *Politics, History and Collective Memory in East Central Europe*. Hamburg: Reinhold Krämer Verlag, pp. 283–291.

Gurrey, Ch. & Munro, N. 2020, 'A Concretisation of Meaning: Making Memorials', in C. Gilbert, K. McLoughlin & N. Munro (eds), *On Commemoration. Global Reflections upon Remembering War*. Berlin: Peter Lang, pp. 197–202.

Hájková, D. & Michela, M. 2018, 'Oslavy 28. října', in D Hájková, P Horák, V Kessler & M Michela (eds), *Sláva republice! Oficiální svátky a oslava v meziválečném Československu*. Praha: Academia, pp. 75–135.

Hájková, D., Horák, P., Kessler, V. & Michela, M. (eds) 2018, *Sláva republice! Oficiální svátky a oslava v meziválečném Československu*. Praha: Academia.

Hájková, D., Horák, P., Kessler, V. & Michela, M. 2018, 'Úvod', in D Hájková, P Horák, V Kessler & M Michela (eds), *Sláva republice! Oficiální svátky a oslava v meziválečném Československu*. Praha: Academia, pp. 13–42.

Halbwachs, M. 1994, *Les cadres sociaux de la mémoire*. Paris: Albin Michel.

Halbwachs, M. 1997, *La mémoire collective*. Paris: Albin Michel.

Havelka, M. 2001, *Dějiny a smysl: obsahy a posuny "české otázky", 1895–1989*. Praha: Lidové noviny.

Hobsbawm, E. & Ranger, T. (eds) 2012, *The Invention of Tradition*. Cambridge: Cambridge University Press.

Holy, L. 1996, *The Little Czech and the Great Czech Nation: National Identity and the Post-Communist Social Transformation*. Cambridge: Cambridge University Press.

Horák, P. 2018, 'První máj', in D Hájková, P Horák, V Kessler & M Michela (eds), *Sláva republice! Oficiální svátky a oslava v meziválečném Československu*. Praha: Academia, pp. 219–266.

Hosking, G. & Schöpflin, G. (eds) 1997, *Myths and Nationhood*. New York: Routledge.

Houžvička, V. 2005, *Návraty sudetské otázky*. Praha: Karolinum.

Hroch, M. 1999, *V národním zájmu*. Praha: Nakladatelství Lidové noviny.

Hroch, M. 2003, *Pohledy na národ a nacionalismus*. Praha: Sociologické nakladatelství.

Hroch, M. 2009, *Národy nejsou dílem náhody*. Praha: Sociologické nakladatelství.

Hrubeš, M. & Navrátil, J. 2017, 'Constructing a Political Enemy: Anti-Communist Framing in the Czech Republic Between 1990 and 2010', *Intersections*, vol. 3, no. 3, pp. 41–62.

Hrubeš, M. & Navrátil, J. 2018, 'Contesting communism after its fall: Anti-communist mobilizations in the Czech Republic between 1990 and 2010', *East European Politics*, vol. 34, no. 1, pp. 1–21.

iROZHLAS 2020, Perspektiva pamětníka a historika definuje střet mezi Klímou a Pullmannem, tvrdí politolog Barša, viewed January 29, 2021, <https://www.irozhlas.cz/zpravy-domov/pullmann-klima-barsa-komunisticky-rezim-ceskoslovensko-identita_2007261729_ktm>.

Jakubec, P. 2013, 'K otázke uznania Slovenského štátu (Slovenskej republiky) Nórskym kráľovstvom, 1939–1940', *Historický časopis*, vol. 61, no. 1, pp. 123–142.

Jarkovská, L. 2020, 'The European Union as a child molester: sex education on pro-Russian websites', *Sex Education*, vol. 20, no. 2, pp. 138–153.

Jeřábek, H., Rössler, J. & Sklenařík, P. 2013, 'Mediální obraz Karla Schwarzenberga v tištěných denících před prezidentskými volbami 2013', *Naše společnost*, vol. 11, no. 2, pp. 3–15.

Judt, T. 2006, *Postwar: A History of Europe Since 1945*. London: Penguin Books.

Kailemia, M. 2016, ' "How do you Say "Stop that!" In Slovakian?": A8 Immigration and Scotland's Race and Ethnic Diversity Narrative', *Sociologia*, vol. 48, no., 3, pp. 247–266.

Khair, T. 2016, *The New Xenophobia*. Oxford: Oxford University Press.

Klíma, M. 2020, Otevřený dopis Michala Klímy členům Spolku studentů historie FF UK, viewed January 29, 2021, < https://www.forum24.cz/otevreny-dopis-michala-klimy-clenum-spolku-studentu-historie-ff-uk/>.

Kluknavská, A. & Smolík, J. 2016, 'We hate them all? Issue adaptation of extreme right parties in Slo-vakia 1993–2016', *Communist and Post-Communist Studies*, vol. 49, pp. 335–344.

Klvaňová, R. 2019, ' "The Russians are back": Symbolic boundaries and cultural trauma in immigration from the former Soviet Union to the Czech Republic', *Ethnicities*, vol. 19, no. 1, pp. 136–155.

Koldinská, M. 2001, 'Válka a všední den. Obraz třicetileté války v každodenním životě české šlechty', *Historie a vojenství*, vol. 50, no. 1, pp. 10–23.

Kopeček, L. 2007, *Politické strany na Slovensku 1989 až 2006*. Brno: Centrum pro studium demokracie a kultury.

Kopeček, L. 2017, *Miloš Zeman. Příběh talentovaného pragmatika*. Brno: Barrister & Principal.

Kopeček, M. 2011, 'The Rise and Fall of Czech Post-Dissident Liberalism after 1989', *East European Politics and Societies and Cultures*, vol. 25, no. 2, pp. 244–271.

Košťálová, P. 2012. *Stereotypní obrazy a etnické mýty: kulturní identita Arménie*. Praha: Sociologické nakladatelství.

Koubová, A. & Poláčková, E. (eds) 2021, *Terény performance*. Praha: Nakladatelství Akademie múzických umění v Praze.

Krasnodebski, Z., Garsztecki, S. & Rüdiger, R. (eds) 2012, *Politics, History and Collective Memory in East Central Europe*. Hamburg: Reinhold Krämer Verlag.

Krasnodebski, Z., Garsztecki, S. & Rüdiger, R. 2012, 'Myth, Lieux de Mémoire, and Collective Memory in Public Discourse', in Z Krasnodebski, S Garsztecki. & R Rüdiger (eds), *Politics, History and*

Collective Memory in East Central Europe. Hamburg: Reinhold Krämer Verlag, pp. 7–17.

Krčál, P. & Naxera, V. 2011, 'Veřejné akce jako divadelní představení', *Central European Political Studies Review*, vol. 13, no. 1, pp. 1–23.

Krčál, P. & Naxera, V. 2015, ' "Díky Ameriko!": dramaturgická analýza Slavností svobody v "nejameričtějším" městě Evropy', *Central European Political Studies Review*, vol. 17, no. 3–4, pp. 313–338.

Krčál, P. & Naxera, V. 2016, ' "Spor bojovníků za svobodu o ideologicky závadný tank": Případová studie tvorby politicky "relevantních" narativ na příkladu plzeňských Slavností svobody v roce 2016', *Central European Journal of Politics*, vol. 2, no. 2, pp. 37–53.

Krčál, P. & Naxera, V. 2019, 'Mýtus svobody: čtyři roky výzkumu Slavností svobody v Plzni', *Střed*, vol. 11, no. 1, pp. 80–101.

Křen, J. 2005, *Dvě století střední Evropy*. Praha: Argo.

Kriegerová, E. 2016, Nový památník připomíná oběti plzeňského květnového povstání, viewed March 8, 2021, <https://www.plzen.eu/o-meste/aktuality/aktuality-z-mesta/novy-pamatnik-pripomina-obeti-plzenskeho-kvetnoveho-povstani.aspx>.

Krotký, J. 2019, 'When Migration Unites Political Parties: The Securitisation of Migration in Czech Party Manifestos', *Politologický časopis*, vol. 26, no. 3, pp. 452–469.

Kubina, L. 2014, 'Oslavy "Prvního máje" v roce 1948: Interpretativní analýzy', *Theatralia*, vol. 6, no. 1, pp. 90–116.

Kulawik, C. & McLoughlin, K. 2020, 'Reconciliation and a Responsibility to the Past', in C Gilbert, K McLoughlin & N Munro (eds), *On Commemoration. Global Reflections upon Remembering War*. Berlin: Peter Lang, pp. 145–149.

Lehnerová, M. 2017, 'Manipulace s kolektivní pamětí na příkladu osvobození Rokycan', *Acta Fakulty filozofické Západočeské univerzity v Plzni*, vol. 9, no. 1, pp. 31–53.

Lentin, R. 2009, 'Memories for the Future', *International Sociology*, vol. 24, no. 2, pp. 173–184.

Liberation Festival 2020, Main page, viewed March 8, 2021, <https://www.slavnostisvobody.cz/>.

Lipset, S.M. & Rokkan, S. 1967, *Party systems and voter alignments: cross-national perspectives*. New York: Free Press.

Lipták, Ľ. 1995, 'Pamätníky a pamäť povstania roku 1944 na Slovensku', *Historický časopis*, vol. 43, no. 2, pp. 363–369.

Lipták, Ľ. 2007, 'Aké dejiny potrebujeme? '*Forum Historiae*, vol. 1, no. 1, pp. 5–11.

Lipták, Ľ. 2008, *Nepřetržité dejiny*. Bratislava: Vydavateľstvo Q111.

Lupták, Ľ. 2008, 'Slovensko: Postkomunismus a národné mýty', in L Cabada (ed), *Nové demokracie střední a východní Evropy*. Praha: Nakladatelství VŠE, pp. 37–65.

Lupták, Ľ. 2010, 'Tvorba Slovenska Maďarskom alebo Ako na seba politické elity cez Dunaj fetišmi mávajú', in L Cabada & P Jurek (eds), *Mentální mapy, teritorialita a identita v evropském prostedí*. Plzeň: Aleš Čeněk, pp. 155–174.

Machcewicz, P. 2012, 'The Institute of National Remembrance and the Legacy of Communism in Poland', in Z Krasnodebski, S Garsztecki & R Rüdiger (eds), *Politics, History and Collective Memory in East Central Europe*. Hamburg: Reinhold Krämer Verlag, pp. 79–97.

Mannová, E. 2008, 'Piruety v inscenování minulosti. Slovenské národní povstání v proměnách času', *Dějiny a současnost*, no 8.

Mannová, E. 2019, *Minulosť ako supermarket? spôsoby reprezentácie a aktualizácie dejín Slovenska*. Bratislava: VEDA.

Mareš, M. 2006, *Symboly používané extremisty na území ČR v současnosti. Manuál pro Policii ČR*. Praha: MInisterstvo vnitra ČR.

Maškarinec, P. & Bláha, P. 2016, 'Křivda jako příležitost pro nové politické strany? Kotleba – Lidové strana Naše Slovensko na cestě do parlamentu', *Politics in Central Europe*, vol. 12, no. 2S, pp. 45–66.

Mayer, F. & Vašíček, Z. 2008, *Minulost a současnost, paměť a dějiny*. Brno: CDK.

Mayer, F. 2009, *Češi a jejich komunismus. Paměť a politická identita*. Praha: Argo.

McLean, I. 2010, 'Political Science and History: Friends and Neighbours', *Political Studies*, vol. 58, pp. 354–367.

Mičev, S. 2020, 'Slovenské národné povstanie a jeho odkaz', in M Syrný (ed), *Slovenské národné povstanie – medzi minulosťou a odkazom pre dnešok*. Banská Bystrica: Múzeum Slovenského národného povstania v spolupráci s Katedrou histórie Filozofickej fakulty UMB v Banskej Bystrici, pp. 5–7.

Michela, M. & Vörös, L. (eds) 2013, *Rozpad Uherska a trianonská mierová zmluva: k politikám pamäti na Slovensku a v Maďarsku*. Bratislava: Historický ústav SAV.

Michela, M. 2008, 'Pripomínanie a kanonizovanie minulosti. Úvaha na margo niektorých diskusií o dejinách Slovenska', *Forum Historiae*, vol. 2, no. 1, pp. 1–13.

Michela, M. 2014, 'Historici a súperenie o podobu nových národných dejín na Slovensku po roku 1989', in R Šustrová & L Hédlová (eds), *Česká paměť. Národ, dějiny a místa paměti*. Praha: Academia, pp. 131–159.

Michela, M. 2017, 'The Struggle for Legitimacy: Constructing the National History of Slovakia after 1989', in O Luthar (ed), *Of Red Dragons and Evil Spirits: Post-Communist Historiography between Democratization and New Politics of History*. Budapest and New York: CEU Press, pp. 115–138.

Michela, M. 2020a, 'Kult osobnosti a legitimizačné stratégie politikov v kontexte osláv SNP v rokoch 1945–1954', *Kulturné dejiny*, vol. 11, pp. 307–328.

Michela, M. 2020b, 'Oslavy výročí Slovenského národného povstania a utvárenie novej socialistickej společnosti v 40.-50. rokoch 20. storočia', in M Syrný (ed), *Slovenské národné povstanie – medzi minulosťou a odkazom pre dnešok*. Banská Bystrica: Múzeum Slovenského národného povstania v spolupráci s Katedrou histórie Filozofickej fakulty UMB v Banskej Bystrici, pp. 25–36.

Mičiniak, P. 2003, 'Geopolitické postavenie Slovenska v rokoch 1939–1941', *Politické vedy*, vol. 6, no. 2, pp. 7–30.

Miháliková, S. 2005, 'Sviatky na Slovensku ako súčásť politických rituálov', *Historický časopis*, vol. 53, no. 2, pp. 339–354.

Miller, D. 2016, *Strangers in Our Midst: The Political Philosophy of Immigration*. Harvard: Harvard University Press.

Mironowicz, E. 2012, 'Belarusian Guerilla Fighters', in Z Krasnodebski, S Garsztecki & R Rüdiger (eds), *Politics, History and Collective Memory in East Central Europe*. Hamburg: Reinhold Krämer Verlag, pp. 221–237.

Moshenska, G. 2020, 'Memorials that Lurk and Pounce', in C Gilbert, K McLoughlin & N Munro (eds), *On Commemoration. Global Reflections upon Remembering War*. Berlin: Peter Lang, pp. 151–156.

Mucha, V. 2009, Chronologie osvobození západních Čech, viewed March 8, 2021, <https://www.aic.cz/osvobozeni/chronologie-osvobozeni-zapadnich-cech-jednotkami-3-u-s-army/>.

Mukhin, Y. 2015, 'Cultural Security of Slovakia in the Context of the Integration of the Slovak Republic in the EU', *Politické vedy*, vol. 48, no. 1, pp. 66–87.

Müller, K.B. 2002, *Češi a občanská společnost*. Praha: Triton.

Müller, K.B. 2016, *Češi, občanská společnost a evropské výzvy*. Praha and Kroměříž: Triton.

Munro, N. 2020, 'Introduction: More than Stone – Finding Ourselves in Our Monuments', in C Gilbert, K McLoughlin & N Munro (eds), *On Commemoration. Global Reflections upon Remembering War*. Berlin: Peter Lang, pp. 113–121.

Musil, J. 1992, 'Czechoslovakia in the Middle of Transition', *Czechoslovak Sociological Review*, vol. 28, pp. 5–21.

Musilová, M. 2014, 'Teatralita veřejných událostí – uvedení do problematiky', *Theatralia*, vol. 6, no. 1, pp. 9–24.

Naxera, V. & Krčál, P. 2016a, 'Obrazy ne-bezpečnosti v projevech slovenských politiků', *Politics in Central Europe*, vol. 12, no. 1S, pp. 49–61.

Naxera, V. & Krčál, P. 2016b, 'Oslavy výročí Slovenského národního povstání v Banské Bystrici v roce 2016 jako legitimizační nástroj představ slovenských politiků', *Acta Fakulty filozofické Západočeské univerzity v Plzni*, vol. 8, no. 2, pp. 29–42.

Naxera, V. & Krčál, P. 2016c, 'The Slovak National Uprising as a national treasure? Interpretation and legacy of the SNU in Slovak political discourse and national mythology', *The Annual of Language & Politics and Politics of Identity*, vol 10, no. 1S, pp. 83–102.

Naxera, V. & Krčál, P. 2017a, 'Perceptions of Slovak Politicians and their Discursive Reification at the Celebrations of the Slovak National Uprising in 2016', *Studia Politica. Romanian Political Science Review*, vol. 17, no. 2, pp. 279–294.

Naxera, V. & Krčál, P. 2017b, 'Všichni proti jednomu? "Anti-kotlebovský" diskurz na oslavách výročí SNP 2017', *Central European Journal of Politics*, vol. 3, no. 2, pp. 26–38.

Naxera, V. & Krčál, P. 2018, ' "This is a Controlled Invasion": The Czech President Miloš Zeman's Populist Perception of Islam and Immigration as Security Threats', *Journal of Nationalism, Memory & Language Politics*, vol. 12, no. 2, pp. 195–215.

Naxera, V. & Krčál, P. 2019, 'The celebrations of the end of the Second World War in the "most American" city in Europe', *Romanian Journal of Political Science*, vol. 19, no. 2, pp. 175–200.

Naxera, V. & Krčál, P. 2020a, ' "How to Sustain National Security": A Case Study of the Celebrations of the Slovak National Uprising as a Securitization Platform', *Social Sciences*, vol. 9, no. 11, pp. 1–13.

Naxera, V. & Krčál, P. 2020b, 'Oslavy výročí Slovenského národního povstání jako platforma pro vytváření obrazů nepřátel Slovenska', *Czech Journal of International Relations*, vol. 55, no. 1, pp. 5–20.

Naxera, V. & Krčál, P. 2020c, ' "Ostrovy deviace" v populistické rétorice Miloše Zemana', *Sociológia*, vol. 52, no. 1, pp. 82–99.

Naxera, V. & Krčál, P. 2021, ' "Čau lidi": performativita politiky', in Koubová, A. & Poláčková, E. (eds), *Terény performance* Praha: Nakladatelství Akademie múzických umění v Praze (in print).

Naxera, V. 2019, ' "Islamophobia without Muslims": Anti-Muslim and anti-Arab Attitudes in Czech Society (Introductory Remarks)', in S Gardocki, R Ozarowski & R Ulatowski (eds), *The Islamic World in International Relations*. Berlin: Peter Lang, pp. 251–267.

Naxera, V. 2021a, 'Sudetoněmecký Landsmanšaft nebo podpora migrace? Německo jako zdroj ohrožení v rétorice Miloše Zemana', *Politické vedy*, vol. 24, no. 3 (in print).

Naxera, V. 2021b, 'The Germans as a threat to 'us'? The use of history and othering of Germans in the speeches of the Czech President Miloš Zeman', in F Jacob & C Schapkow (eds), *Nationalism and Populism. Expressions of Fear or Political Strategies?* Berlin: De Gruyter (manuscript).

Naxera, V., Glied, V., Filipec, O. & Kaczorowska, M. 2020, ' "To protect national sovereignty from the EU?" The 2019 EP elections and populist parties in V4 countries', *Revista UNISCI*, vol. 54, pp. 71–106.

Nečasová, D. 2020, *Obrazy nepřítele v Československu 1948–1956*. Praha: Nakladatelství Lidové noviny.

Nora, P. 1989, 'Between Memory and History: Les Lieux de Mémoire', *Representations*, no. 26, pp. 7–24.

Nora, P. 2010, 'Mezi pamětí a historií: problematika míst', in F Mayer, A Bensa & V Hubinger (eds), *Cahiers du CEFRES. Antologie francouzských společenských věd: Město*. Nové Město: CEFTES, pp. 39–63.

Oláh, G. 2013, 'Kolektivní paměť, prostor a významy. Případ náměstí Svobody v Budapešti', *Sociologický časopis*, vol. 20, no. 2, pp. 30–34.

Olick, J.K., Vinitzky-Seroussi, V. & Levy, D. (eds) 2011, *The Collective Memory Reader*. Oxford: Oxford University Press.

Overing, J. 1997, 'The Role of Myth: An Anthropological Perspective, of: The Reality of the Really Made-Up', in Hosking, G. & Schöpflin, G. (eds), *Myths and Nationhood*. New York: Routledge, pp. 1–18.

Pakhomenko, S. & Gridina, I. 2020, 'Securitization of Memory in the Pandemic Period: The Case of Russia and Latvia', *Czech Journal of International Relations*, vol. 55, no. 4, pp. 94–116.

Paměť národa, Undated, Díky, Ameriko! viewed February 24, 2021, < https://www.mistapametinaroda.cz/?id=567&lc=cs>.

Pažur, Š., Chmelárová, M. & Halaj, D. 1979, *Odkaz SNP*. Bratislava: Osveta.

Phillips, A.L. 2001, 'The Politics of Reconciliation Revisited: Germany and East-Central Europe', *World Affairs*, vol. 163, no. 4, pp. 171–191.

Pitař, M. 2012, 'Trianonská smlouva a její reflexe v současné maďarské politice', *Acta Fakulty filozofické Západočeské university v Plzni*, vol. 4, no. 3, pp. 121–143.

Plzeň 1945, 2008, Cesta k osvobození, viewed March 8, 2021, <http://plzen1945.cz/?p=1565>.

Portmann, K. 2018, ' "Jednou Němec. Vždycky Němec". Německy mluvící obyvatelstvo v Československu po druhé světové válce', in J Pažout & N Portmann (eds), *"Nechtění" spoluobčané. Skupiny obyvatel perzekvovaných či marginalizovaných z politických, národnostních, náboženských i jiných důvodů v letech 1945–1989*. Prague and Liberec: ÚSTR and TUL, pp. 28–42.

Pullmann, M. 2008, 'Sociální dějiny a totalitněhistorické vyprávění', *Soudobé dějiny*, vol. 15, no. 3–4, pp. 703–717.

Pullmann, M. 2011, *Konec experimentu. Přestavba a pád komunismu v Československu*. Praha: Scriptorium.

Rak, J. 2018, 'The Typological Framework of Myths as a Tool for Studying Political Thought', *World Political Science*, vol. 14, no. 2, pp. 1–22.

Randák, J. & Koura, P. (eds) 2008, *Hrdinství a zbabělost v české politické kultuře 19. a 20. století*. Praha: Dokořán.

Randák, J. 2008 'Historie v současném i budoucím veřejném prostoru – úvahy o dějinách a paměti', *Forum Historiae*, vol. 2, no. 1, pp. 14–22.

Rawls, J. 2006, *Political Liberalism*. New York: Columbia University Press.

Roediger, H.L., Abel, M., Umanath, S., Schaffer, R.A., Fairfield, B., Takahashi, M. & Wertsch, J.V. 2019, 'Competing national memories of World War II', *Proceedings of the National Academy of Sciences of the United States of America*, vol. 119, no. 34, pp. 16678–16686.

Rosputinský, P. 2016, 'K otázke štátnosti Slovenského štátu/Slovenskej republiky', *Acta Fakulty filozofické Západočeské univerzity v Plzni*, vol. 8, no. 1, pp. 75–100.

Roučka, Z. 2005, *...a přinesli nám svobodu*. Plzeň: ZR & T.

Said, E. 1978, *Orientalism*. New York: Pantheon Books.

Schmitt, C. 1932, *The Concept of the Political*. Chicago: University of Chicago Press.

Schwarzmantel, J. 2008, *Ideology and Politics*. London: Sage.

Sendyka, R. 2016, 'Sites That Haunt: Affects and Non-sites of Memory', *East European Politics and Societies and Cultures*, vol. 30, no. 4, pp. 687–702.

Sereda, V. 2012, 'The Symbolic Landscape of Lviv', in Z Krasnodebski, S Garsztecki & R Rüdiger (eds), *Politics, History and Collective Memory in East Central Europe*. Hamburg: Reinhold Krämer Verlag, pp. 359–385.

Siegel, M. & Harjes, K. 2012, 'Disarming Hatred: History Education, National Memories, and Franco-German Reconciliation from World War I to the Cold War', *History of Education Quarterly*, vol. 52, no. 3, pp. 370–402.

Šima, K. 2017, 'Od rituálů a obyčejů k performancím aneb jak studovat festivity moderní doby?', *Studia Ethnologica Pragensia*, vol 8, no. 1, pp. 17–49.

Skilling, G.H. 1970, 'Thaw and Freeze-Up: Prague 1968', *International Journal: Canada's Journal of Global Policy Analysis*, vol. 25, no. 1, pp. 192–201.

Slačálek, O. 2010, 'Boj o národ. Obrazy Mnichova ve sporech o českou zahraniční politiku', *Czech Journal of International Relations*, vol. 45, no. 4, pp. 51–70.

Slačálek, O. 2018, 'Morální panika a její kritici', *Central European Journal of Politics*, vol. 4, no. 4, pp. 4–33.

Smith, A. 1997, 'The "Golden Age" and National Renewal', in G Hosking & G Schöpflin (eds), *Myths and Nationhood*. New York: Routledge, pp. 36–59.

Sniegon, T. 2017, *Vanished History: The Holocaust in Czech and Slovak Historical Culture*. New York: Berghahn Books.

Stanislav, J. 2020, 'Širšie súvislosti nacistickej okupácie Slovenska a postoj ludáckej garnitúry k povstaniu', in M Syrný (ed), *Slovenské národné povstanie – medzi minulosťou a odkazom pre dnešok*. Banská Bystrica: Múzeum Slovenského národného povstania v spolupráci s Katedrou histórie Filozofickej fakulty UMB v Banskej Bystrici, pp. 8–19.

Staniszkis, J. 1999, *Post-communism: the emerging enigma*. Warsaw: Polish Academy of Sciences.

Strážay, T. 2005, 'Myths in Action: Two Cases from southern Slovakia', in Z Hlavičková & N Maslowski (eds), *The Weight of History in Central European Societies*. Prague: CES, pp. 101–113.

Strukov, V. & Apryshchenko, V. (eds) 2018, *Memory and Securitization in Contemporary Europe*. London: Palgrave Macmillan.

Švecová, M. 2020, 'Regime Preferences in Communist Czechoslovakia and the Narrative on the Slovak National Uprising', *Political Preferences*, vol. 27, pp. 79–94.

Syrný, M. (ed) 2020, *Odkaz Slovenského národného povstania*. Banská Bystrica: Múzeum Slovenského národného povstania v spolupráci s Katedrou histórie Filozofickej fakulty UMB v Banskej Bystrici.

Szaló, C. 2017, *Paměť míst. Kulturní sociologie vzpomínání*. Praha: Sociologické nakladatelství.

Tampke, J. 2003, *Czech-Germans Relations and the Politics of Central Europe*. London: Palgrave Macmillan.

Tomczuk, S.J. 2016, 'Contention, consensus, and memories of communism: Comparing Czech and Slovak memory politics in public spaces, 1993–2012', *International Journal of Comparative Sociology*, vol. 57, no. 3, pp. 105–126.

Toušek, L., Lupták Burzová, P., Růžička, M. & Dvořáková, I. 2014, *Karlov mezi industriální a postindustriální společností*. Plzeň: Západočeská univerzita v Plzni.

Valko, R. 2020, 'Deformácie výkladu SNP v rokoch 1949–1960', in M Syrný (ed), *Slovenské národné povstanie – medzi minulosťou a odkazom pre dnešok*. Banská Bystrica: Múzeum Slovenského národného povstania v spolupráci s Katedrou histórie Filozofickej fakulty UMB v Banskej Bystrici, pp. 37–44.

Verdery, K. 1999, *The Political Lives of Dead Bodies*. New York: Columbia University Press.

Violi, P. 2012, 'Politics of Memory. Tuol Sleng, Villa Grimaldi and the Bologna Ustica Museum', *Theory, Culture & Society*, vol. 29, no. 1, pp. 36–75.

Voda, P., Kluknavská, A. & Spáč, P. 2021, 'Electoral Success of the Extreme Right Party ĽSNS in Slovakia', *Problems of Post-Communism*, online first.

Williams, K. 1997, 'National Myths in the New Czech Liberalism', in G Hosking & G Schöpflin (eds), *Myths and Nationhood*. New York: Routledge, pp. 132–140.

Wingfield, N.M. 2000, 'The Politics of Memory: Constructing National Identity in the Czech Lands, 1945 to 1948', *East European Politics and Societies*, vol. 14, no. 2, pp. 246–267.

Wittenberg, J. 2015, 'Conceptualizing Historical Legacies', *East European Politics and Societies and Cultures*, vol. 29, no. 2, pp. 366–378.

Wyss, J. 2020, 'Stones Do Not Forget: Forgetting and Being Forgotten in Czech Silesia', in C Gilbert, K McLoughlin & N Munro (eds), *On Commemoration. Global Reflections upon Remembering War*. Berlin: Peter Lang, pp. 225–229.

Zákravský, J. 2017, *Baskové v ofsajdu. Sport jako nástroj politiky nestátních národů. Případová studie fotbalu v Baskicku*. Praha: Dokořán.

Zombory, M. 2017, 'The birth of the memory of Communism: memorial museums in Europe', *Nationalities Papers*, vol. 45, no. 6, pp. 1028–1046.

Žúborová, V. & Borárosová, I. 2016, 'Migrácia v médiách: utečenci verzus migrant. Chápanie migrantov a utečencov v mediálním priestore v kontexte pozitívnej a negatívnej mediatizácie', *Central European Journal of Politics*, vol. 2, no. 1, pp. 1–15.

Žúborová, V. & Borárosová, I. 2017, 'Migration Discourse in Slovak Politics. Context and Content of Migration in Political Discourse: European Values versus Campaign Rhetoric', *Journal of Nationalism, Memory & Language Politics*, vol. 11, no. 1, pp. 1–19.

www.ingramcontent.com/pod-product-compliance
Lightning Source LLC
Chambersburg PA
CBHW070310230426
43664CB00015B/2705